Case Studies in eLearning

For Researchers, Teachers and Students

Edited by

Sue Greener

Case Studies in eLearning
Volume One
First published: November 2013

ISBN: 978-1-909507-81-4

Copyright © 2013 The authors

All rights reserved. Except for the quotation of short passages for the purposes of critical review, no part of this publication may be reproduced in any material form (including photocopying or storing in any medium by electronic means and whether or not transiently or incidentally to some other use of this publication) without the written permission of the copyright holder except in accordance with the provisions of the Copyright Designs and Patents Act 1988, or under the terms of a licence issued by the Copyright Licensing Agency Ltd, Saffron House, 6-10 Kirby Street, London EC1N 8TS. Applications for the copyright holder's written permission to reproduce any part of this publication should be addressed to the publishers.

Disclaimer: While every effort has been made by the editor, authors and the publishers to ensure that all the material in this book is accurate and correct at the time of going to press, any error made by readers as a result of any of the material, formulae or other information in this book is the sole responsibility of the reader. Readers should be aware that the URLs quoted in the book may change or be damaged by malware between the time of publishing and accessing by readers.

Note to readers.
Some papers have been written by authors who use the American form of spelling and some use the British. These two different approaches have been left unchanged.

Published by: Academic Publishing International Limited, Reading, RG4 9SJ, United Kingdom, info@academic-publishing.org
Printed by Ridgeway Press

Available from www.academic-bookshop.com

Contents

Contents i
List of Contributors iii
Introduction to Case Studies in eLearning v
Technical, Methodological or Psychological Preparation: a Case Study of Using Electronic Portfolio Assessment in Initial Teacher Education in Hong Kong 1
Jane Mok

The Changing Roles of Staff and Student Within a Connectivist Educational Blog Model 18
Elaine Garcia, Mel Brown and Ibrahim Elbeltagi

"Digital Futures in Teacher Education": Exploring Open Approaches towards Digital Literacy 36
Anna Gruszczynska, Guy Merchant and Richard Pountney

The Yin/Yang of Innovative Technology Enhanced Assessment for Promoting Student Learning 62
Maggie Hutchings, Anne Quinney, Kate Galvin and Vince Clark

E-Enablement in Distance Education – Engineering Growth: A Case Study of IMT-CDL 80
Tushar Marwaha and Anita Mathew

Learning Analytics Artefacts in a Cloud-Based Environment: A Design Science Perspective 103
Phelim Murnion and Markus Helfert

eLearning: Tool to Ensure Growth and Sustainability of SMEs 122
Andrée Roy

Sharing and Shaping Effective Institutional Practice in TEL Through the 3E Framework 141
Keith Smyth

Challenges in Developing e-Submission Policy and Practice 160
Alice Bird

Case Studies in eLearning

Tools for Evaluating Students' Work in an Interactive (Open) Virtual Space: Case Study of an eLearning Course in an International Network of Universities...178
Jana Dlouhá, Martin Zahradník, Jiří Dlouhý and Andrew Barton

Mutlimodal Teaching Through ICT Education: An e-Twinning Program as a Case Study of Intercultural Exchange..200
Paraskevi Kanari and Georgios Potamias

List of Contributors

Andrew Barton, Charles University Environment Center, Prague, Czech Republic
Alice Bird, Liverpool John Moores University, UK
Mel Brown, Plymouth College of Art, UK
Vince Clark, Bournemouth University, UK
Jana Dlouhá, Charles University Environment Center, Prague, Czech Republic
Jiří Dlouhý, Charles University Environment Center, Prague, Czech Republic
Ibrahim Elbeltagi, University of Plymouth, Plymouth, UK
Kate Galvin, Bournemouth University, UK
Elaine Garcia, Plymouth College of Art, UK
Sue Greener, University of Brighton, UK
Anna Gruszczynska, Sheffield Hallam University, UK
Markus Helfert, School of Computing, Dublin City University, Dublin, Ireland
Maggie Hutchings, Bournemouth University, UK
Paraskevi Kanari, National Kapodistrian University of Athens, Greece
Tushar Marwaha, IMT-Centre for Distance Learning, Ghaziabad, UP, India
Anita Mathew, IMT-Centre for Distance Learning, Ghaziabad, UP, India
Guy Merchant, Sheffield Hallam University, UK
Jane Mok, The University of Hong Kong, Hong Kong
Phelim Murnion, School of Business, Galway-Mayo Institute of Technology, Galway, Ireland
Georgios Potamias, National Kapodistrian University of Athens, Greece
Richard Pountney, Sheffield Hallam University, UK
Anne Quinney, Bournemouth University, UK
Andrée Roy, Université de Moncton, Moncton, Canada
Keith Smyth, Edinburgh Napier University, UK
Martin Zahradník, Charles University Environment Center, Prague, Czech Republic

About the author

Dr Sue Greener is Principal Lecturer at the University of Brighton Business School teaching Learning & Development, HRM, Business Context and Research Methods and has received a Teaching Excellence award from the University. She is Programme Leader for the consortium FdA Business, Business Pathway Leader for Joint Honours Degree and Course Leader for BSc Business with Enterprise. Sue is also the Course Director for a fully online final year undergraduate course with students in diverse world regions. She researches, advises and supervises in the fields of e-learning strategy, Technology Enhanced Learning and reflective learning. Sue is the co-founder of the Business e-Learning Research Group and a member of the CROME and CIMER research groups at Brighton Business School. She is Editor of the academic journal Interactive Learning Environments, published by Routledge. Sue holds a BA, MBA, EdD, FHEA and is a Chartered Fellow of CIPD.

Nobody likes to be a guinea pig, but everyone likes innovation.

Introduction to Case Studies in eLearning

As technologies change our working patterns, our leisure and our learning activities in daily life, we strike positions on the technology adoption scale which show our greater or lesser degree of enthusiasm for technological change. Some of us are out and out enthusiasts, never happier than when we are trying out new gadgets or apps and coming up with new uses for these novelties in the way we contribute to learning. However, most learning practitioners are a little more cautious; not against the new, but concerned that short-term ideas could be adopted for the sake of novelty rather than as a considered response to genuine opportunities for learning and teaching. Where is the pedagogic justification, we cry? Well, this book is a collection of papers which answer that cry. Each has endeavoured to contextualise and justify the innovation demonstrated, and each has built upon pedagogic theory to offer a considered view of the ideas described.

All the case studies here discuss innovations based on technologies for enhancing learning. Each describes the challenges, benefits and limitations of the innovation, and often their entailed complexities. At the same time, the very nature of the content means that we are dealing here with students and staff as "guinea pigs" who have experimented with technologies and who may not always be happy with the experience. This particularly applies when the experiments are driven by institutional decision-makers with little consultation, but even small-scale innovations at modular or project level can strike the actors in the experiment as unnecessary, or as following trends rather than considered approaches to improving the way we learn and teach.

So the case studies in this collection have been chosen to represent a wide range of technologies, educational contexts and subject disciplines with the intention of presenting a state of the art picture from recent e-learning conferences. Here are the collected endeavours of a group of folk who urgently believe in the changes they discuss, and who have gone to considerable trouble to justify, evaluate and share their ideas and experiences for the benefit of the learning and teaching community. We have case studies based in countries from Atlantic Canada to Poland and Greece, set in young and older school-age groups, universities and workplaces. Research methodologies used include qualitative methods such as narrative analysis, interviews, surveys and social research, plus quantitative methods including learning analytics. Learning technologies explored include blogging tools, wikis, e-portfolios, computer-assisted assessment, audience response surveys through mobile devices, social media tools, peer review and grading software, Cloud-based computing and multimedia projects. Issues addressed include blended learning, e-submission, institutional frameworks for technology enhanced learning, power relations between stakeholders of change, collaborative learning and the use of Open Educational Resources. A cornucopia of experiences.

The case study format is of vital importance for practitioners, especially those who want to adopt new practices and technologies but who face a whole range of practical or pedagogic questions for which they seek answers before following the innovators. Where new or changing phenomena are experienced, and this clearly relates to the world of learning technologies, it is so helpful to read of specific projects, associated with the practical data of time, number, delivery and outcomes which can help teachers assess the justification for change in their own circumstances. Cases allow evidence to be presented and tested by those engaged with applying and developing new ideas. Certainly they will not all offer generalizability, but what they lose here, they gain in accessibility to a wide readership (Nisbet & Wyatt 1984). Most of the studies in this book are of the exploratory or narrative kind (Yin 2000). They set out a clearly delineated example of educational practice which we can use to benchmark our own practice and identify trend movements in learning and teaching, offering us all a map for this new territory.

Sue Greener

Today's teaching and learning experience is a challenging one, but perhaps this has always been the case. There is a sense in which control is shifting away from teachers to learners, while at the same time quality assurance measures increase preparation requirements and over-focus on specific learning outcomes, taking us away from a wider, more open-ended learning experience in education. Teachers praise the virtues of self-directed independent learning, and this is a genuine goal for Higher Education in particular, yet they may not yet have fully faced the implications of students who can, with ease, shop around for input from other teachers at other institutions through their smartphones. Teachers who excel at delivering face-to-face lectures will always find themselves in demand both offline and online, but not all teachers have that skill and feel threatened by Massive Open Online Courses, video-recordings of high status figures in their field, and those whose facility with information and communications technology may appear way ahead of their own. A number of the case studies in this collection discuss the notion of digital literacy and explore how different conceptions of digital skills, learning approaches and processes are affecting our understanding of effective learners and teachers.

This book demonstrates that innovations do not come singly. The authors establish in paper after paper that not only the specific innovation or pilot study discussed in the case demonstrates creativity and challenge, but that frequently the context of learning and teaching for these cases is also of itself innovative. Simply reading through the cases as a range of strongly innovative learning experiences is a humbling but positive experience, let alone exploring the specific innovations evidenced in these contexts. Take, for example, the case study from Hutchings *et al* (2012), which discusses innovative assessment strategies, but at the same time is based in the context of a highly innovative second year undergraduate module. That module involves web-based case studies, narratives, poems, published research, videos and policies supplemented by lectures and group work. This seems to suggest that e-learning research practitioners tend to have an innovation mindset, rather than being focussed on single interventions, and they are likely to be the authors of series of innovations which lead their colleagues into experimentation.

Many of these cases discuss the tensions and divergent perspectives of learning technologies: for example the paper from Gruszczynska *et al* (2012) who present competing perspectives of digital literacy and Bird (2011) who presents competing stakeholder perspectives of a major cultural shift when introducing e-submission. How hard is it then, for teachers to introduce technological innovations to enhance learning? For the last ten years it has been relatively easy to gain opportunities for such innovation, given determination and an acceptance of considerable up-front preparation on top of normal teaching loads. However, these case studies suggest that the field of e-learning is developing in maturity; that there is much more experience on which to draw, and much more critical and considered comment on the impacts and relevance of such innovation. Some believe that the objective is to lose sight of the technology and just be aware of the improvements in learning enabled by it. Others see added affordances of value from learning with technology which need to be recognised, not hidden. Perhaps ultimately we may have to accept that the nature of learning is changing: not just for younger people, but for all. As we struggle with information overloads, information filters are growing in popularity, making user-friendly decisions for us as to what we should find from search engines, and what we want to read at any particular time. As teachers and researchers in e-learning, we are becoming increasingly aware of the pitfalls of connectedness as well as the benefits related to learning in community. Technology is both reducing in visibility at the same time as mounting a takeover in our freedom to learn. It is through documenting each innovation through case studies such as those in this collection, that we document this revolution and resist the role of "guinea pig".

Sue Greener
November 2013
University of Brighton, UK

References
Nisbet, J., & Watt, J., (1984) Case Study, Chapter 5 in Bell, K., et al (Eds), Conducting Small-Scale Investigations in Educational Management, London: Harper & Row
Yin, R. K. (2009) Case Study Research: Design and Methods, (4th Edition). California, SAGE Publications.

Technical, Methodological or Psychological Preparation: a Case Study of Using Electronic Portfolio Assessment in Initial Teacher Education in Hong Kong

Jane Mok
Division of English Language Education, Faculty of Education, The University of Hong Kong, Hong Kong

> **Editorial Commentary**
> Set in Hong Kong, this case study explores how student teachers work with e-portfolios as part of their own assessment. The paper considers the affordances of e-portfolios as places to capture the development of thought and learning, offering control over this journey to the learner. As so often with innovation involving learning technology, the researchers grapple with support issues to make quite sure the e-portfolio tool is fit for purpose. What, for example, do you do with a series of e-portfolios – where and how do you store them, how do you assess potentially lengthy pieces of work, and how do you ensure that students less competent at strong visual presentation and design are not unduly penalised, when creative design is not the subject discipline in which they study? In comparing e-portfolio use over two cohorts, this study offers the kind of research practitioner learning which is so valuable for teachers who wish to innovate but can get side-tracked by the detail of the innovation and lost sight of the aim and the actors within the change.

Abstract: A major challenge for language teacher educators working in the area of language awareness is to develop pedagogical and assessment approaches that will go beyond merely enhancing L2 teachers' subject-matter knowledge by enabling them to make the bridge between the declarative and procedural dimensions of teacher language awareness. In this paper, we discuss on-going efforts at the University of Hong Kong to design assessment tasks for the language awareness course entitled 'Pedagogical Content Knowledge'. The final-year student-teachers taking the course are required to compile an electronic portfolio based on their reflections on the relevance and applicability of the issues relating to dealing with the content of learning in pedagogical practice discussed in the course. As Lynch and Purnawarman (2004:50) point out, 'a solid electronic portfolio can show reflection, evolution of thought and overall professional development'. Research shows that electronic portfolio assessment can successfully engage learners in critical thinking and problem solving, promote lifelong education, encourage self evaluation and allow learners to have a higher degree of control over the learning process (Pierson and Kumari, 2000; Mason, Pegler, and Weller, 2004). Given the value of electronic portfolios, growing interest has been seen in using electronic portfolio assessment to support teacher education (Lynch and Purnawarman, 2004). The paper sets out to describe and analyze issues relating to the design and implementation of the assessment, focusing specifically on the challenges the research team faces. The case study shows that apart from technical support, psychological and methodological preparations are also needed to help students to perform effectively in the computer-supported assessment. In our paper, we will be drawing on a range of data, including excerpts from students' electronic portfolios and their feedback on the assessment to critically evaluate the extent to which the assessment has succeeded in achieving the intended learning outcomes. Implications are drawn for those who plan to conduct electronic portfolio assessment in higher education.

Keywords: electronic portfolio assessment, psychological preparation, methodological preparation, assessment innovation, teacher education

1. Introduction

Advances in technology have certainly enhanced our living in many different ways. With the help of technology we can now communicate easily with others through different multimedia systems. We can also search for and have access to different kinds of information from the Internet. Technology has indeed been making a difference in various important aspects of our lives including communication and education. In terms of education, for example, the online discussion forum, if implemented thoughtfully, has been found to successfully engage learners outside the classroom (Balaji and Chakrabarti, 2010), and to promote reflection and interaction among learners (Downing and Chim, 2004). With enhanced features such as flexibility in storage, production and dissemination (Barrett, 2000), the introduction of electronic portfolio has taken portfolio assessment in education to a new level.

In this paper, the research/teaching team discusses reflectively ongoing efforts at the University of Hong Kong to design assessment tasks for a teacher language awareness course. The student-teachers of L2 English taking the course are required to develop electronic portfolios based on their reflections on the applicability of the issues relating to dealing with different language systems in pedagogical practice discussed in the course. The paper sets out to describe the significance of portfolio and electronic portfolio assessment in education. The implementation process of the electronic portfolio assessment in the course is then detailed. A range of data, including the patterns that emerged in the electronic portfolios collected, student-teachers' feedback on the assessment as well as the reflections of the tutors, are drawn to critically evaluate the extent to which the assessment has succeeded in achieving its intended learning outcomes.

2. Literature review

Portfolios, as defined in this study, are 'rich, contextual, highly personalized documentaries of one's learning journey. They contain purposefully organized documentation that clearly demonstrates specific knowledge, skills, dispositions and accomplishments achieved over time. Portfolios represent connections made between actions and beliefs, thinking and doing, and evidence and criteria. They are a medium for reflection through which the builder constructs meaning, makes the learning process transparent and learning visible, crystallizes insights, and anticipates future direction' (Jones and Shelton, 2011: 21-22). The portfolio building processes that learners go through engage them in a reflective inquiry process (Zubizarreta, 2004) and provide them with a holistic learning experience (Jones and Shelton, 2011), which helps explain why different forms of portfolios and portfolio assessment have been widely adopted in the educational context worldwide (Kinnard, 2007).

The potential benefits of portfolio assessment have well been documented in the education literature. For example, the self-directing and on-going natures of the assessment such as learners collecting and selecting items to be included in the portfolio, seeing connections between these artifacts and reflecting on them over a period of time (Mason, Pegler and Weller, 2004) encourage reflection, self evaluation and critical thinking (Pierson and Kumari, 2000), and develop in the learners a sense of voice (Jones and Shelton, 2011) and ownership of learning (Zubizarreta, 2004). All of these benefits were the reasons why portfolio assessment was adopted when the language awareness course was first introduced. To better prepare the student-teachers of L2 English for the literacy pedagogy challenge, that is, 'it now must account for the burgeoning variety of text forms associated with information and technologies' (The New London Group, 2000: 9), the paper portfolio assessment was replaced by electronic portfolio assessment in the following academic year.

On top of all the benefits of paper portfolio assessment, electronic portfolio assessment offers learners a multimedia platform to design, produce and distribute their portfolios e.g. learners can enhance their portfolios using a combination of digital media including animation and sound effects (Kilbane and Milman, 2005). It indeed allows learners with greater flexibility in terms of both capturing the items to be reflected on, storing of the artifacts, and duplicating and distributing their portfolios (Barrett, 2000). According to Jones and Shelton (2011: 145), the 'non-linear structure [of electronic portfolios] means that support documentation can be virtually attached where appropriate without compromising the overall community and flow of the document'. Specifically, in the context of teacher education, electronic portfolio assessment could engage student-teachers with the use of technology so as to develop their digital literacy (Lane, 2009). As in this case study, one of the intended learning outcomes of the electronic portfolio assessment was to develop student-teachers' understanding of the interplay between various types of knowledge including content, pedagogical and technological knowledge.

Despite their benefits, portfolio and electronic portfolio assessments present challenges to both their implementers and builders. According to Parsons (1998), portfolio assessment needs to be approached with caution to ensure success. Janesick (2011: 42) also points out that 'although teachers and students get into the computer age and all that it requires, one can image that the transition to electronic portfolios is gradual and not necessarily easy'. In terms of the implementers, issues such as technical training for both staff and students, problems with portfolio archiving, and increased workload of faculty, all need to be dealt with properly. The issues of technology and time are two determining factors that need to be addressed in relation to both the implementer and builder alike (Zubizarreta, 2004).

According to Kinnard (2007), the process of constructing a portfolio is complex and it consists of three major phrases: introspective, design and implementation. In the context of teacher education, the first stage involves student-teachers reflecting introspectively their teaching beliefs and practices with respect to the focus of the portfolio assessment. In the next two stages, the processes of collecting items to be included in the portfolio, selecting and categorizing them, and recording related reflections will continue until the artifacts are actually arranged and presented in the portfolio. These processes especially those involved in electronic portfolio building could be novel to many student-teachers and thus methodological support is needed to help them commit in this, time-consuming and possibly daunting, portfolio building process. In terms of psychological support, Parsons (1998) stresses that learners need to be helped to see the active role they play in the 'new' learner-centred assessment, and be empowered to negotiate their voices and identities in order to perform effectively in the assessment.

3. Implementation of the assessment

3.1. The teacher language awareness course

The course to which electronic portfolio assessment was introduced is part of an initial teacher education programme that integrates English study, education, English language teaching methodology and school experience. The course aims to develop the teacher language awareness of student-teachers of L2 English as it relates to different language systems such as grammar, lexis and phonology. According to Thornbury (1997: x), teacher language awareness refers to the knowledge that teachers have of the 'underlying systems of the language that enables them to teach the subject effectively'. In other words, the language-aware EFL teachers, as in this case study, need to be able to reflect on their knowledge about language, and their knowledge of the learner, and draw appropriately on their knowledge about language in all aspects of his or her pedagogical practice (Andrews, 2007) to enhance language teaching and learning. An important principle underpinning the curriculum design of the course is to prioritize student-teachers' development of metacognitive awareness so as to help them assess their own knowledge about language, evaluate their own pedagogical decisions and performance and modify their teaching assumptions and practices. The assessment task for the course aims to provide these student-teachers with opportunities to capture and reflect on their own experiences of dealing with different language systems and to re-evaluate some of their content-related pedagogical decisions in light of the knowledge gained on the course. Electronic portfolio assessment was first introduced to the course to replace paper portfolio assessment in 2009/2010 to facilitate student reflection and digital literary development. This paper compares the extents to which the assessment had achieved these two intended learning outcomes in 2009/2010 and 2010/2011.

3.2. The student-teachers

There were two sub-classes of student-teachers taking the language awareness course in 2009/2010 (i.e. 21 and 25 student-teachers in sub-classes A and B respectively) and 2010/2011 (i.e. 22 and 19 student-teachers in sub-classes A and B respectively). Although all of the students from the two cohorts had been using different social networking sites e.g. Facebook, to communicate with each other, they did not have the experience of building their own electronic portfolios. Many of them lacked the technical knowledge or skills for video editing, which was indeed a prerequisite for developing their electronic portfolios for the course. Most of them admitted that they had not heard about the University recommended portfolio building software, Mahara, before the course. Some student-teachers from the 2009/2010 cohort were found to be reluctant to log on to the new faculty e-learning platform from which they could access Mahara. Student-teachers from the two cohorts were asked on various occasions their comments on the electronic portfolio assessment implemented in the course, e.g. the end-of-term teaching evaluation survey and their feedback is reported in this paper. As there was a change in tutor in sub-class A in 2010/2011, only the implementation process of the assessment in sub-class B is detailed and compared to maintain continuity. The patterns that emerged in the 25 and 19 electronic portfolios submitted by the student-teachers in sub-class B in 20019/2010 and 2010/2011 are also examined in detail in this study.

3.3. The 2009/2010 cohort

The 25 student-teachers in sub-class B of the 2009/2010 cohort were given a large amount and various kinds of technical input to conduct the electronic portfolio assessment. Specifically, a technical staff member was assigned to support their electronic portfolio building process. Technical support in the forms of manuals, in-class demonstrations, and technical support hotlines was provided to help the student-teachers complete and submit their assignments. In each electronic portfolio, student-teachers had to include two pieces of reflections detailing their teacher language awareness development, a brief contextual description of their teaching practice school and classes as well as a few extended pieces of reflections on the course online discussion forum, the teaching materials they used, the student compositions they marked and two content-related incidents that they captured in video during their practicum. They were encouraged to be creative when constructing their electronic portfolios. Although some difficulties were encountered such as the files and video clips included in some electronic portfolios could not be opened properly, all the student-teachers in the sub-class managed to submit their assignments before or shortly after the deadline. Based on their format, the 25 electronic portfolios submitted can be grouped under five different categories (see Table 1 in section 3.4): (1) all the files such as Word, video and PPT are uploaded as attachments to the electronic portfolio, (2) one or more Word files is/are uploaded as attachments with the video files in the ready-to-show format as required, (3) one or more Word files is/are uploaded as attachments with ready-to-show video clips, and images of student work and textbook materials being reflected on, (4) text, ready-to-show video clips, and images of student work and textbook materials, and (5) text, ready-to-show video clips, images of student work and textbook materials, and other enhanced features such as photos, graphics and sound effect.

Regarding the question on students' perceptions of the new assessment in the end-of-term course evaluation survey, based on the 24 questionnaires returned from the whole cohort (i.e. 46), the electronic portfolio assessment has been rated 3.13 on its usefulness under a 5-point likert scale with 5 representing very useful. The result was somewhere between the highest rating, 3.63, on the course tutorials and teaching materials, and the lowest rating, 3.08, on the online discussion forum introduced to the course in the same year. In terms of student feedback, while some student-teachers complained about the heavy workload of the course, others expressed the need to have clearer instructions for the assessment task. On the whole, the whole cohort of student-teachers held rather negative opinions on developing their portfolios electronically and/or Mahara. One student stated in the questionnaire that the 'non-text format [assignment] is not preferred' and another considered things like video trimming 'unrelated' to their studies. All of their comments on the electronic portfolio assessment are listed below:

Workload

- *too much for the E-portfolio*

- *less coursework*

- *less coursework would be better*

Instructions

- *need clearer instructions for assignments. Perhaps a sample/ template.*

- clearer guidelines are preferred

- guidelines about assignments are very unclear, not sure what I am expected

Mahara

- it might be more convenient to submit the video with DVDs than through Mahara

- Mahara is too difficult to use!

Developing the portfolio electronically

- trimming video and presenting in non-text format is not preferred

- should not expect Ss to do unrelated things e.g. trim videos, presenting in non-text format

In terms of the intended learning outcomes of the assessment, that is, facilitating student-teachers' digital literacy development, with only 17 student-teachers managed to present their ideas properly in their electronic portfolios (i.e. types 4 and 5), the research team believed that the primary aim to develop student-teachers' digital literacy through electronic portfolio assessment had barely been achieved. Only 2 electronic portfolios, among the 25 submitted, were, to some extent, technically enhanced, that is, including features that could not be integrated in traditional paper portfolios. A student-teacher included in his portfolio a piece of self-composed music to remember the learning process he went through in the course and another student-teacher integrated an animation showing a pen writing out her final self-evaluation of teacher language awareness in the portfolio. Regarding developing the metacognitve awareness of the student-teachers, based on the in-depth reflections of the declarative and/or procedural dimension(s) of teacher language awareness shown in the portfolios submitted, the aim to enhance the metacognitive awareness of the student-teachers had been achieved.

3.4. The 2010/2011 cohort

19 electronic portfolios were submitted by the student-teachers in sub-class B in 2010/2011. In terms of content, the requirements for their electronic portfolios were exactly the same as those of the 2009/2010 cohort. However, support and preparation with different focuses e.g. psychological, technical and methodological were given to this sub-class at different stages. In terms of psychological preparation, at the beginning of the academic year, the tutor went through with the sub-class the components and criteria of the electronic portfolio assessment, assuring that they would be provided with all kinds of support they needed to build their electronic portfolios. Also, they were explained the significance of electronic portfolio assessment e.g. to help develop their digital literacy, and why it was adopted in the course, e.g. to address the issue of storing different types of artifacts including video clips of classroom teaching, and to provide them with greater flexibility in terms of the design and production of their electronic portfolios.

Regarding technical support, after the meaning of teacher language awareness was explored and discussed in the course, each student-teacher in the sub-class was asked to write down his/her initial self-evaluation of teacher language awareness on a piece of patterned paper provided by the tutor. The reflections were then scanned, transformed into PDF files, and returned to the student-teachers. The tutor then showed the sub-class how they could upload their PDF files onto Mahara to make their reflections the very first item required in the electronic portfolio. Most of the student-teachers were indeed happy that they could follow the instructions easily and they were encouraged to explore different uploading functions and presentation options on Mahara at their own time.

The student-teachers were then methodologically prepared for the assessment. They were advised to create a specific folder and sub-folders to save up all the possible artifacts for their portfolios including drafts of their reflections. Specific attention was drawn to the importance of constantly evaluating, reflecting on and selecting appropriate artifacts for their portfolios over the course period. The tutor highlighted also the uniqueness and ownership of the portfolios, trying to help the student-teachers see the important and active role they played in the new assessment. The student-teachers were then asked what specific technical support they would hope to have before the submission. The requested support was given to the sub-class about one month before the deadline of the assessment.

All the student-teachers in this sub-class managed to present their ideas properly in their electronic portfolios (i.e. types 4 and 5). Based on their format, the 19 electronic portfolios can be grouped under two different categories (see Table 1 below): (a) text, ready-to-show video clips and image(s) of initial self-evaluation of teacher language awareness (and teaching materials being analysed), and (b) text, ready-to-show video clips, image(s) of initial self-evaluation of teacher language awareness (and student work and textbook materials being analysed), and other enhanced features such as photos, graphics and sound effect. The submission process was smooth and some student-teachers indeed submitted their portfolios days before the deadline. The technician went through each submitted portfolio carefully e.g. viewing all the files attached, before sending the student-teacher involved an email to acknowledge the receipt of the portfolio.

Table 1: Electronic portfolios submitted by sub-class B

	2009/2010 cohort	2010/2011 cohort
(1) All the files (Word, video and PPT) are uploaded as attachments to the electronic portfolio	2	0
(2) All the Word files (one or multiple) are uploaded as attachments with the video files in the ready-to-show format as required	4	0
(3) All the Word files (one or multiple) are uploaded as attachments with ready-to-show video files, and images of student work and textbook materials being reflected on	2	0
(4) Text, ready-to-show video clips, and image(s) of initial self-evaluation of teacher language awareness (and teaching materials being analysed)	9 *	6

	2009/2010 cohort	2010/2011 cohort
(5) Text, ready-to-show video clips, and image(s) of initial self-evaluation of teacher language awareness (and teaching materials being analysed) and other enhanced features	8	13
Total	25	19

* The video clips in one of the electronic portfolios in this category were not in the ready-to-show format.

Regarding the question on students' perceptions of the new assessment in the end-of-term course evaluation survey, based on the 37 questionnaires returned from the whole cohort (i.e. 41), the electronic portfolio assessment has been rated 3.22 on its usefulness, slightly higher than the one from the year before (i.e. 3.13). The result was somewhere between the highest rating, 3.69, on the micro-teaching component of the language awareness course, and the lowest rating, 3.05, on the course online discussion forum. In terms of student feedback, while some student-teachers in the whole cohort continued to complain about the heavy workload of the course and to express their dislike of the electronic portfolio assessment, one piece of positive feedback was received, that is a student-teacher could see the benefit of doing portfolio assessment electronically stating that this new format was 'environmental friendly'. In fact, two student-teachers told the tutor in their assignment feedback session that they had enjoyed the electronic portfolio building process and did not find it difficult. All the feedback collected from the end-of-term evaluation questionnaires are listed below:

Positive comment(s) on the assessment

- The electronic portfolio is environmental-friendly.

Negative comment(s) on the assessment

- Too much work to do throughout the course.

- I don't prefer using e-portfolio as the form of assessment as it is difficult to manage.

- I think submitting either hard copies of the portfolio or the e-portfolio could yield the same learning outcomes, and I could not see the advantages of submitting the final assignment as an e-portfolio instead of the hard copies.

- I think the electronic portfolio is very time consuming and it doesn't contribute to my learning of this course. I prefer handing in hard copy

With all 19 student-teachers managed to present their in-depth reflections on teacher language awareness in their electronic portfolios (i.e. types 4 and 5), the research team believed that both intended learning outcomes of the assessment had been achieved in the academic year 2010/2011. In fact, three student-teachers were able to enhance further their electronic portfolios by using effectively the multi-media platform provided. A student-teacher included in his portfolio different short video clips of him introducing various components of the portfolio. Another student-teacher included in her portfolio songs and video clips relating to her learning and teaching. Last but not least, a student-teacher included a theme song and a flip book in her portfolio to summarize her final self-evaluation of teacher language awareness. The tutor was happy to see the improvements shown in this sub-class.

4. Discussion

The findings show that the research/teaching team was too occupied by various technical challenges and issues in relation to the implementation of the electronic portfolio assessment that they had not prepared the 2009/2010 sub-class psychologically and methodologically for the new assessment (Mok, 2011). Psychologically, they had not helped the student-teachers see the underlying principle of the assessment e.g. allowing them much flexibility in capturing, presenting and storing their experiences in dealing with different language systems for reflection, and they had not, in any way, elicited from the student-teachers their needs or concerns regarding the new assessment before or during the implementing process. Most importantly, they had not even explained to the student-teachers why the portfolio assessment had to be done electronically. The student-teachers were not prepared psychologically, in any way, for the new assessment experience.

Methodological 'preparation [that] involves the acquisition of the necessary knowledge and techniques that will enable the learner to fulfil his role' (Kolláth, 1996: 311) effectively in the new assessment was also not available to the student-teachers in this sub-class. They were not explained how they could approach the assessment for example by saving all the possible artifacts in a designated place for further reflection and selection. The lack of methodological and psychological preparations could have contributed to some student-teachers' negative and insecure feelings for the assessment. As revealed in some portfolios submitted (i.e. types 1-3), some of the student-teachers indeed did not show any intention to compose their portfolios electronically. And, even if some did, they seemed to lack the skills to do it effectively despite the tremendous technical support given to them. What is shown seems to reflect an attitude problem with the student-teachers, i.e. a lack of commitment in creating their portfolios electronically.

In terms of the psychological and methodological preparations that this sub-class could have needed, the recommendations that Hargreaves and Fullan (1998) make regarding taking advantage of the power of emotional resources of students to help them learn in the context of educational change could be applicable. These include getting students motivated by helping them understand the underlying principles of the new assessment, using different support strategies to raise their comfort level and involving them as much as possible in the change process. As in 2010/2011, the tutor explained explicitly to the student-teachers the benefits and principles of the new assessment, built with them step by step their electronic portfolios in class and invited them to voice their concerns especially the support that they would hope to have regarding the new assessment during its implementation process. All of these strategies seem to have impacted positively on the 2010/2011 student-teachers and thus enhanced their commitment in developing their portfolios electronically (i.e. only types 4 & 5 portfolios were submitted in the academic year). A few student-teachers even reported to have seen the advantage of the new assessment and enjoyed the electronic portfolio building process.

Apart from walking the student-teachers through the electronic portfolio building process, the research/teaching team has also been trying to establish stronger links between the new assessment with the course curriculum and the faculty e-learning platform since 2010/2011, making the electronic portfolio assessment also an assessment for learning task. For example, student-teachers were invited to share their drafts of reflective essays on the e-learning platform to invite feedback from their group-mates and tutor. They were then encouraged to reflect on and improve their essays continuously throughout the course period. The active role they played in the assessment and the uniqueness of their portfolios were also highlighted in the implementation process e.g. they can decide on what to include in their portfolios and how they are going to present them. The various measures have helped the student-teachers in 2010/2011 see the importance and advantages of doing the portfolio assessment electronically and better prepared them for the new assessment experience.

5. Conclusion

This case study reveals that the student-teachers in 2010/2011 were better prepared psychologically, technically and methodologically than those in 2009/2010 regarding the electronic portfolio assessment, which in turn maximized its learning potential. The findings point to the need for teachers to be aware of the importance of student preparation in implementation of assessment innovations (Mok, 2011). The study, though exploratory, has important implications regarding the implementation of electronic portfolio assessment. First of all, various types of student support e.g. psychological, methodological and technical may be needed to help students to perform effectively in the assessment. Secondly, in terms of psychological preparation students need to be shown the significance of the assessment before they could commit whole-heartedly in the time-consuming and possibly challenging electronic portfolio building process.

In terms of educational and/or assessment innovations regarding e-learning, the study shows that it is important for the implementer to understand that technical support is not all that learners need. On top of psychological and methodological preparation, it takes time for learners as well as teachers to understand and learn about any educational innovation. Last but not least, it is important for teachers to put learners' experience in the heart of the change process e.g. by listening to the concerns they have about the change. Future research investigating the implementation process of e-learning innovations needs to be conducted so as to maximize their learning potential. The research/teaching team hopes that the paper facilitates further exchanges of ideas and reflections on the use and implementation of electronic portfolio assessment in the educational context.

References

Andrews, S. (2007) Teacher language awareness, Cambridge: Cambridge University Press.

Mok, J. (2011) 'A case study of students' perceptions of peer assessment in Hong Kong', ELT Journal, vol 65, no 3, pp.230-239.

Barrett, H. (2000) How to Create Your Own Electronic Portfolio, [Online], Available: http://electronicportfolios.org/portfolios/howto/index.html [16 January 2012].

Balaji, M. S. and Chakrabarti, D. (2010) 'Student interactions in online discussion forum: Empirical research from 'media richness theory' perspective', Journal of Interactive Online Learning, vol. 9, no. 1, pp. 1-22.

Downing, K. and Chim, T.M. (2004) 'Reflectors as online extraverts', Educational Studies, vol. 30, no. 3, pp. 265–276.

Hargreaves, A. and Fullan, M. (1998) What's worth fighting for out there, New York: Teachers College.

Janesick, V. J. (2011) Stretching exercises for qualitative researchers, 3rd edition, Thousands Oaks: Sage.

Jones, M. and Shelton, M. (2011) Developing your portfolio: Enhancing your learning and showing your stuff, New York: Routledge.

Kilbane, C. R. and Milman, N. B. (2005) The digital teaching portfolio workbook: Understanding the digital teaching portfolio development process, Boston: Allyn and Bacon.

Kinnard, J. (2007) From crayons to cyberspace: Creating a professional teaching portfolio, Belmont, CA: Thomson Higher Education.

Kolláth, K. (1996) The Importance of Learner Training as a Tool to Develop Autonomous Learners, [Online], Available: http://elib.kkf.hu/okt_publ/szf_06_33.pdf [16 January 2012].

Lane, C. (2009) 'Technology and change', in Cambridge, D, Cambridge, B. and Yancey, K. B. (ed.) Electronic Portfolios 2.0: Emergent Research on Implementation and Impact, Sterling, Virginia: Stylus.

Mason, R., Pegler, C. and Weller, M. (2004) 'E-portfolios: An assessment tool for online courses', British Journal of Educational Technology, vol. 35, no. 6, pp. 717-727.

Parsons, J. (1998) 'Let us proceed with caution', Adult Learning, vol. 9, no. 4.

Pierson, M. and Kumari, S. (2000) 'Web-based student portfolios in a graduate instructional technology program', in Willis, D., Price, J. and Willis, J. (ed.) Technology and Teacher Education Annual 2000, Charlottesville, VA: Association of Computers in Education.

The New London Group. (2000) 'A pedagogy of multiliteracies: designing social futures', in Cope. B. and Kalantzis, M. (ed.) Mutliliteracies: Literacy Learning and the Design of Social Futures, London: Routledge.

Thornbury, S. (1997) About language, Cambridge: Cambridge University Press.

Zubizarreta, J. (2004) The learning portfolio: Reflective practice for improving student learning, San Francisco: Jossey-Bass.

The Changing Roles of Staff and Student Within a Connectivist Educational Blog Model

Elaine Garcia[1], Mel Brown[1] and Ibrahim Elbeltagi[2]
[1]Plymouth College of Art, Plymouth, UK
[2]University of Plymouth, Plymouth, UK

Editorial Commentary

Blogging is being increasingly adopted in Higher Education as the benefits of reflection and collaboration which the blog potentially offers are recognised as relevant to students' learning as well as continuing professional development for staff. Blogging software offers granularity in the levels of connection which can be made both internally within an educational institution and beyond its boundaries. So a case study which focusses on developing understanding of the theoretical concepts underpinning blog production and ensuing dialogue is of great interest. An application of the theory of Connectivism, which is discussed in this case study, has continuing relevance to educators facing an increasingly connected and less didactic role in Higher Education. Similarly, students can adopt blogging to develop, not just connections outside the university environment and across their subject discipline, but also to build their own personal learning network, community and environment for learning. Collective blogging, which was used in the module studied here, offers particular opportunities for learners to take on self-directed, independent stances in relation to their learning with staff attending more to the process of learning than the content input. However, blogging activities do not necessarily produce even results for all learners, suggesting a continuing role for learning experts and facilitators.

Elaine Garcia, Mel Brown and Ibrahim Elbeltagi

Abstract: Whilst the use of web 2.0 tools and specifically blogs is becoming increasingly popular within Higher Education (HE) and has been shown to promote learning (Garcia, Brown & Elbeltagi, 2012) relatively little is known about the manner in which such tools may affect the roles of both staff and students within teaching and learning. It is within this context that connectivism, a learning theory for the digital age, provides a model through which the roles of staff and students when using collective student blogs for teaching and learning can be considered. Within this research a case study of a collective student blog project, undertaken by students based within an HE institution, is utilised to explore the changing nature of the roles of both staff and students through a connectivist-learning model of blog usage. From this case study it would appear that connectivism does provide a sound theoretical model for the way in which staff and student roles may change as a result of the use of blogs within teaching and learning. However the experience of staff and students who undertook the project suggests that whilst a number of elements of the connectivist model can be identified, these are not seen universally amongst all students. Where a connectivist model of learning through blogs can be seen to be effective, staff were considered to be able to be more constructively critical in their feedback whilst being less directly involved in formative feedback to the student, which was welcomed by staff. Students meanwhile also considered benefits to exist and these largely related to the manner in which students were able to provide and receive peer review and feedback in a more critical and constructive way than they had before, seeing the benefits this could provide. These benefits were however dependent upon other group members also responding in a timely and constructive manner.

Keywords: blogs, connectivism, higher education, changing academic staff roles, changing student roles

1. Introduction

The use of Web 2.0 within Higher Education (HE) has become increasingly popular in recent years and consequently much has been written concerning the manner in which such tools can be used to enhance teaching and learning. What has been less clearly articulated however is the manner in which such tools can fundamentally change student and staff roles, not only as a result of the use of technology but also the effect that the use of such tools has on how learning occurs. This has led, particularly through the use of blogs, to the development of new forms of teaching, learning, pedagogy and learning theories.

One of the most relevant theories, to come to prominence due to the rise of Web 2.0 is Connectivism. Connectivism is not an area in which a great deal of research has been conducted particularly in relation to the use of blogs within teaching and learning and the effect the use of blogs may have on both staff and student roles. The roles of both staff and students are particularly important within a connectivist-learning model and this is therefore an area that requires further investigation.

Before considering the extent to which blogs reflect a connectivist-learning model and the manner in which this affects staff and student roles, in terms of both teaching and learning, it will be first necessary to consider the nature of connectivism as a teaching and learning theory before considering the manner in which this will be reflected in the use of blogs for teaching and learning.

2. Connectivism

The learning theory of connectivism was developed as a result of a belief that there was a need for a learning theory, which took into account the manner in which society has changed as a result of the new technologies of the digital age. (Siemens, 2004)

Connectivism is driven by the influence of social constructivism, network theory and chaos theory (Couros, 2009) and highlights the importance of learners making connections, which allow the flow of information to occur between the learner and their learning community. (Kop & Hill, 2008)

Within a connectivist-learning environment, learners use technology to create networks for themselves, which are open and filled with information sources that the individual chooses. This makes the network highly personalised and the responsibility of the individual. (Guder, 2010) As a result individuals are required when building their network to consider what information is of importance and what information is not. The ability of learners to additionally be able to judge when a network may no longer be useful are also vital elements of connectivism. (Siemens, 2004)

Siemens (2004) defines the key principles of connectivism as follows:

- Learning and knowledge can rest in diversity of opinion
- Learning is a process of connecting specialised nodes or information sources
- Learning can reside in non-human appliances
- Capacity to know is more critical than what is currently known
- Nurturing and maintaining connections is needed to facilitate continual learning
- Ability to see connections between thoughts, ideas and concepts is a core skills
- Currency is the intent of all learning activities
- Decision making is itself a learning process

It is clear within connectivist learning that the individual and their network is of key importance. In addition the nature of the network appears to support a fundamental change in the role of academic staff as when they are present within a learner network (although this cannot be assumed) their role will be of a peer. (Friesen & Lowe, 2011)

Within this approach learning is seen to occur when peers collaboratively share opinions, viewpoints and critiques through conversation and dialogue on a more mutual basis than the traditional teacher / student relationship. (Friesen & Lowe, 2011)

In addition it is important to note that within a connectivist-learning model does not only take place within the classroom but also outside of it, often made possible due to mobile digital technologies (Guder, 2010) and the connections formed with others who may wish to continue to learn outside of the classroom.

The nature of the networks formed also places the emphasis for making and choosing connections on the student rather than the teacher. (Guder, 2010) This therefore places a greater emphasis on the student's role within the learning process and where it exists the teachers role will be determined by the learner rather than the teacher. (Guder, 2010)

This theory is however not without its critics. Verhagen (2006) has been critical of connectivism, as he does not consider it to be a learning theory as it is based at a curriculum level rather than an institutional level. Verhagen (2006) therefore believes connectivism should be considered a pedagogy rather than a learning theory. This criticism is further support by Kerr (2007) who considers that something interesting is happening but that this is not necessarily at the level of a learning theory. Furthermore Kerr (2007) also considers that issues arise from connectivism when consideration is taken of "non-universals" which are things, which are not learnt spontaneously such as reading and writing. Despite these criticisms the concept of connectivism continues to be considered of relevance when considering learning within the digital age.

3. Connectivism and blogs

The use of blogs would appear to support connectivist learning due to the manner in which blogs are considered to provide opportunities for individuals to collaborate and communicate online with others. (Richardson, 2010) Furthermore blogs enable the creation of social structures (Efimova & Hendrick, 2005) particularly where collective blogs are used as a learning tool.

Collective blogs provide many of the features considered to be of importance in a connectivist-learning model such as allowing interaction, (Ferdig & Trammell, 2004) peer and social communities to be promoted to support learning, (Glogoff, 2005) and a continuity of conversation. (Macduff, 2009) Whilst the use of blogs can be therefore seen to meet the needs of a connectivist-learning model it is important to consider the effect this will have on staff and student roles.

Initially it must be noted that in order for blogs and a connectivist approach to be adopted staff must firstly be willing and able to use such tools. (Kvavik, 2005) As it is usually the decision of staff to use the specific technologies within a session there will be a need for staff to have knowledge of such technologies. However whilst academic staff may need knowledge of the technology the manner in which control of both the digital and learning environment moves from staff to students is an important distinction to make within both student blogs and connectivist learning. This therefore changes the role of both staff and student, particularly within group student blogs where students become accountable to each other rather than the teacher. This therefore places the role of the teacher as one concerned with ensuring that students are actively engaged and responding in a timely and relevant way to each other's posts rather than replying themselves. (Livingston, 2011) This will however be difficult to achieve if blogs are busy or large numbers of students are involved.

The connectivist model and nature of blogs also supports any time, any place learning which may suit students but may not be appropriate for staff who may be unable to be available on a flexible basis. (Lujan-Mora & Juana-Espinosa, 2007)

One further aspect of blogging that would well support the connectivist-learning model is the manner in which external "experts" could become involved within the blog more easily than in an offline environment. The nature of blogs and the ability to reach audiences across the Internet also allows students to focus on specific communities that may be most relevant to them. The manner in which students, staff and experts may interact within the connectivist-learning blogging model is shown in figure 1.

Figure 1 demonstrates the relationships that exist between students within the blogging environment and the manner in which staff and experts may input into the community but are not automatically involved within the learning environment.

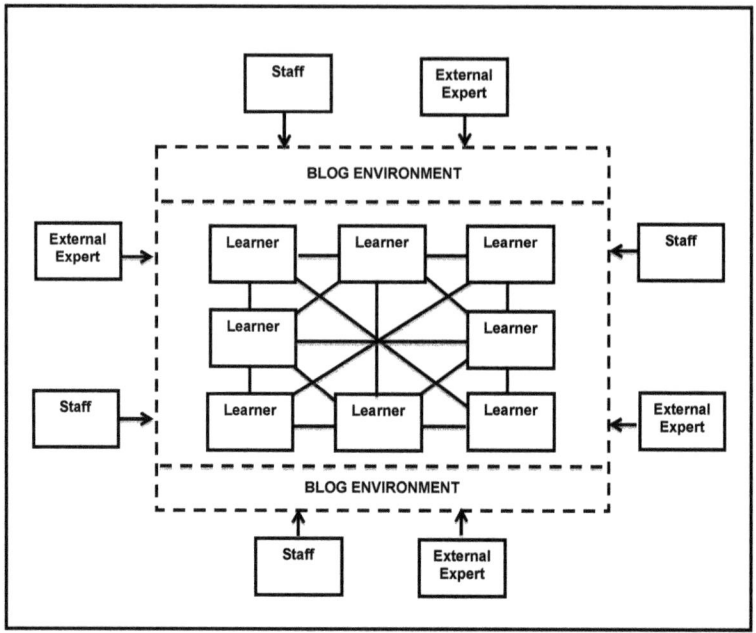

Figure 1: Connectivist educational blog model

In order to determine the extent to which this model represents a realistic interpretation of the use of blogging within teaching and learning, the case study of Plymouth College of Art (PCA) shall now be considered.

4. Methodology

The research is undertaken using a qualitative approach. This approach is considered to be most useful in this case as it allows the collection of research data within a natural setting and seeks to gain an understanding of participants and the relationships that exist between participants. (Saunders, Lewis & Thornhill, 2012)

According to Creswell and Clark (2011) the advantages of such an approach include:

- It aims to describe and interpret participant's personal experiences of a phenomena
- It allows participants to share their view
- It provides a way of understanding complex phenomena
- It tries to understand the interactions between people

This therefore helps to ensure that the validity of the results is relatively high. (Creswell, 2009)

4.1. Case study method

A case study is a qualitative research method, which allows the researcher to explore phenomena within context. (Saunders, Lewis & Thornhill, 2012) Case studies are a useful method where a researcher wishes to gain a detailed understanding of the context in which the phenomena is occurring. (Saunders, Lewis & Thornhill, 2012) One of the key advantages of a case study is the manner in which it can deal with a variety of evidence (Saunders, Lewis & Thornhill, 2012). By using a variety of evidence a more detailed view of the phenomena can be considered. (Yin, 2009)

4.2. Data analysis

A total of 33 students and the academic staff team (2 staff) were asked to complete a survey, which utilised open-ended questions. In addition the staff team wrote both personal and team reflection throughout the project and were interviewed following the project. Student surveys were returned from members of five of the six teams (IJ, TF, FFF, TI and WWSY). In addition results from both staff interviews (ST1) and staff surveys (ST2) were received.

The results of both the interviews and qualitative written responses were analysed using narrative analysis. This method was chosen as it allows an account of the experience individuals have to be told in a sequential manner, which allows the opportunity to explore the events, which may be related to each other and which may provide an indication of areas of importance for researchers. (Saunders, Lewis & Thornhill, 2012)

5. Case study

The BA (Hons) Illustration course is a three-year degree programme, which runs at PCA. The use of collective student blogs occurs within a module called "Illustrative Practices" within the second year of the course. Within this module, a simulated work based learning project called "The Great Editorial Race" runs for three weeks. This project requires students to work in groups to create a number of illustrations in a relatively short timespan. The course team assigns teams and each team is responsible for setting up a group blog. A total of six teams were created and each was assigned by staff in order to be evenly distributed in terms of characteristics and performance.

The aim of the blog was to create a flexible, asynchronous online space in which students could post ideas, research and sketches, which could be commented on by others in the team before submission. This space would not be an area in which academic staff would actively participate as it was hoped that the blog would enable students to create an online community that would provide peer support and build on offline activities undertaken in the studio.

6. Findings

6.1. Student views of the changing nature of academic / student roles

From the qualitative surveys conducted it would appear that through the use of collective blogs students did appear to make connections with others as would be expected within a connectivist-learning model:

> "They were very valuable... They were all positive and friendly and made you feel part of a team and not working all alone" (IJ1)

Furthermore it appears that students found the connections made within the blog provided a supportive environment in which critique, comment and constructive feedback was given therefore allowing learning to occur:

"It was really helpful in deciding what improvements to make." (TF1)

"It is reassuring. Letting me know I'm going in the right direction and am valued by the group." (FFF1)

This appeared to be considered by students to be driven by the student rather than by academic staff and where feedback was given it appears that this was often considered to be constructive and useful:

"We were all honest and appreciated useful feedback as to why certain things were not working." (WWSY1)

However whilst this reportedly occurred in some cases this success was not universal and did not occur automatically or immediately:

"At first we were all too polite, but before the end we had relaxed a bit and were still positive, but offering proper feedback." (IJ1)

For some students the academic staff role was required initially within the project in order to initiate discussion and critical feedback:

"We needed prompting to use it as more than a "look at what I've done!" blog and were giving each other constructive comments towards the end." (IJ1)

This appeared to be for some students an issue of confidence in their own opinions and the ability to share their views with other students.

"I found the comments valuable but I think because of the 'newness' of the group it was a bit difficult to be completely honest. Also I'm sure that one's opinions are only subjective, so I did not want to comment on the blog, lest it be misunderstood – would have preferred to discuss it in person with the others on a one to one basis." (FFF1)

Whilst therefore it appears that the connectivist environment and blogs appeared to work well for some students the success of the blogs was not universal and whilst some blogs saw interaction from all of the group:

> "Everyone actively left comments and feedback within good time" (TF1)

A number of students commented that posts and responses often came from the same students:

> "Comments were usually from the same people it would have been nice to have feedback from all members." (WWSY1)

> "Some members were active and some were not. It was the inactive that concerned me." (TF2)

This might therefore provide an indication that not all students were actively engaged or learning through collective blogs and therefore the connections required for learning to occur were not sufficiently strong. This manifested not just through lack of engagement but also through a lack of timely engagement. For example:

> "A lot of people in our group didn't post their work up on the blog until it had been submitted leaving no opportunity for other people from the group to suggest improvements." (WWSY1)

It is important to note that for some students the technology itself appeared to be an issue and not all participants appeared to embrace the technology:

> "We tended to do more in class/face to face than on blog...we did (show really early ideas) in person so no point in doing on blog for the sake of it." (TI1)

It is important to note that whilst some students considered that face-to-face communication replaced online communications it is worth noting that all teams discussed using a variety of methods of communication.

Overall therefore it appears that students found connections, although to varying degrees, within the blogs and were able to use these to learn.

"We all used the team blog to display and discuss work as it progressed. It allowed us to critique each other and make suggestions." (TF1)

Whilst the views of students have been considered it is necessary to consider the manner in which staff felt both their own and student roles changed as a result of the use of technology.

6.2. Staff Views of the changing nature of academic / student roles

From the staff results it is evident that academic staff felt their role within this project had changed from their usual role:

"The teaching team "played" the role of art director rather than tutor throughout…. Although students could approach staff for art direction whenever they wished only a handful of students took this opportunity consistently." (ST1)

In this way therefore the academic staff considered that they were no longer:

"…Automatically the first port of call for asking for advice and feedback (as students) have to use each other for feedback outside of the classroom to get feedback on their own ideas through peer critique." (ST2)

Lecturers therefore considered that students were largely self-managing their learning and considered that:

> *"Students not only learn individual skills in terms of working to briefs but they also develop critical thinking and reflection skills in terms of critiquing their own and others work."* (ST1)

However whilst this generally worked well it did result in a loss of critical review that students might receive, as students were *"sometimes just too polite."* (ST2)

This therefore reflects the views of students who noted that peers were too polite and did not wish to be critical of each other although it appears this became less of an issue as connections between individuals became strengthened through interaction:

> *"The blogs setup for the race were not continued after the game had ended…and most students returned to their own peer group of friends to discuss their work."* (ST1)

This may therefore indicate that connections made were not strong or enduring or were perhaps not of high value to students. Alternatively however within a connectivist-learning model this could be expected as the specific relevance of the network did not necessarily exist any longer and so students choose to revert or build new networks.

Within this case study academic staff did not consider themselves to become part of the learning group but instead remained on the edges of the learning process and did not become peers as suggested within a connectivist model. Additionally however staff did not consider themselves to be removed from the learning process entirely:

> *"There was still a sense that we were still seen as authority figures with the race – setting the work, judging the editorials, providing critical feedback."* (ST1)

Staff considered that the lack of engagement by some students within the blog could affect the success of the project and the learning that occurs:

"It is clear that some students learnt so much more from the blog than others largely because as a whole group they were ensuring the blogs worked effectively for them. There's that moment when an effective online critiquing community is completely dependent on that need for that community to be fully engaged." (ST1)

Overall it would appear that academic staff considered their role did change to some extent as a result of blog usage. This however does not appear to entirely meet the expectations of the connectivist model of learning. The implications of these findings shall therefore be considered in more detail in terms of both the changing roles of staff and students as a result of the use of blogs.

7. Discussion

From the findings it is clear that both staff and students consider that the use of blogs within this project had a fundamental impact, not only in terms of the increased opportunities the technology allowed for collaboration and interaction, but also in terms of the roles students and staff held.

From both staff and student views a connectivist learning model appeared to be largely delivered through the use of blogs, as students were empowered to create peer communities and communicate, collaborate and interact using technology. However unlike the connectivist model, it is important to note that student groups were not self-initiated and networks did not form or grow organically outside of the groups staff assigned.

It would appear therefore that academic staff maintained an authoritative role within the learning process and whilst not engaging within the blog, as would be expected within a connectivist-learning model, were still looked to as an authoritative source of learning by students.

It would certainly appear that within this model the responsibility for learning did become more focused toward the student and the peer group however students did not appear to be able to fully engage with the level of peer critique and feedback that appears to be required in such a model although it did occur in some cases.

In terms of the role of staff it appears that the use of technology represented no barrier, as staff initiated the choice of such tools. It should be noted however that whilst staff had no input into the blogs themselves the selection of the tool as a suitable medium required an understanding of the capability of the tool.

The academic role in this case appeared to largely relate to the creation of the learning opportunity and the judging of final work as opposed to the usual guidance staff would give students throughout. This therefore placed a greater emphasis on the need for peer assessment and feedback.

Students who engaged with the task appeared to benefit, particularly as confidence grew and critiquing became easier. Where some students failed to engage, staff noted that this negatively affected the learning of all within the group. Within this case study staff did not check the engagement of students and therefore self-managed groups needed to be accountable for themselves, something which students perhaps found hard to adapt to, especially initially.

Overall it would appear that blogs do reflect many of the principles of a connectivist-learning environment and largely was a successful model in this case. In terms of the student role the need for students to take responsibility for their own learning and the creation of their own networks have on the whole occurred successfully and learning occurred as a result. Students however still appeared to look to staff as authority figures and appeared to do little to extend, manage or continue the network following the project.

Within a connectivist-learning model the manner in which staff would be expected to not be directly involved in student learning networks or involved only as a peer did appear to occur to some extent but not entirely. Staff were still required to play an authoritative role in the learning process although there does appear to be a degree of greater freedom for academic staff to be removed from each individual student's learning process and to be able to critique on a more formal basis. For academic staff this role allowed a greater focus for students on the need for self-reflection and peer critique and this in turn allowed staff the opportunity to become removed from the individual learning process although not from the group learning activity.

8. Conclusions and recommendations

This research has examined the manner in which staff and student roles can be considered to change when using a connectivist-learning blog model. This study has found that the roles of staff and students clearly change as a result of the use of blogs and these would largely appear to meet the expectations of a connectivist learning model but not entirely.

The findings from this case study would suggest that the use of blogs results in a student role which is more focused towards seeking and providing peer-critique, support and guidance and as a result there is a need for students to be fully engaged and willing participants within group learning. The student role in this model therefore becomes increasingly concerned with self-management and a need to take greater responsibility for individual learning, which does not necessarily occur naturally.

For academic staff, roles also appear to change as a result of the use of blogs in a connectivist model. Due to the changes seen in student roles, academic staff become less involved in the individual learning process of each student and instead focus on providing the opportunities for learning and overall summative critique at the end of the task. This change will also not necessarily occur naturally and may need to be practised and refined by staff.

Whilst the changes in roles demonstrate that some elements of connectivism can be seen within this case study it is clear that these roles identified were not adopted in all cases, particularly amongst students. As a result some students may have failed to actively or fully engage with the project and consequently their level of learning may have been affected. This is likely to be resolved if the project were assessed and this would need to be carefully considered in the future when setting such activities.

From this case study it is possible to see that blog usage has had a positive effect on both staff and student roles and the learning that took place. However this was a relatively short project following which students appeared to disengage with the blogs created. The result of this case study therefore suggests a need for further empirical research to be conducted within this area.

Further research may consider the use of blogs within a longitudinal study, within other disciplines and with greater student numbers. In terms of a connectivist-learning model, the use of blogs should be continued and the use of external experts and self-organised groups could be utilised in order to further develop the positive changes seen in both student and staff roles.

References
Couros, A. (2009) Open, connected, social – implications for educational design, *Campus-wide Information Systems*, Vol. 26, no. 3, pp232-239.
Creswell, J. (2009) Research Design – Qualitative, Quantitative, and Mixed Methods Approaches, 3rd Edition, Sage Publications: USA
Creswell, J. & Clark, V. (2011) Designing and conducting mixed methods research, Sage Publications: USA
Downes, S. (2005) An Introduction to Connective Knowledge, [Online] http://www.downes.ca/post/33034, [Accessed 15/05/12]
Efimova, L. & Hendrick, S. (2005) In search for a virtual settlement: An exploration of weblog community boundaries. Communities and Technologies.
Ferdig, R. & Trammell, K. (2004) Content Delivery in the "Blogosphere" *THE Journal Online*, Vol. 2004, Feburary.
Friesen, N., & Lowe, S. (2011) The questionable promise of social media for education: connective learning and the commerical imperative, *Journal of Computer Assisted Learning*, Vol. 28, no. 3, pp183-194.
Garcia, E., Brown, M. & Elbeltagi, I. (2012) The Effectiveness of Collective Group Blogs as a Tool for Reflection within Experiential Learning Projects: A Case Study of Simulated Work Based Learning within Higher Education, Proceedings of the *International Technology, Education and Development (INTED)*, Valencia, March 5-7 2012, pp4676-4685, IATED

Glogoff, S. (2005) Instructional Blogging: Promoting interactivity, student-centred learning, and peer input, *Innovate,* Vol. 1, no. 5.

Guder, C (2010) Patrons and Pedagogy: A Look at the Theory of Connectivism, Public Services Quartley, Vol. 6, no. 1, pp36-42

Kerr, B (2007) A Challenge to Connectivism, [Online], http://learningevolves.wikispaces.com/kerr, [Accessed 22/05/12]

Kop, R., & Hill, A. (2008) Connectivism: Learning theory of the future or vestige of the past?, The International Review of Research in Open and Distance Learning, Vol. 9, no. 3.

Kvavik, R. (2005) Convenience, Commincations, and Control: How Students Use Technology. In Oblinger, D. & Oblinger, J. (eds), *Educating The Net Generation,* pp7.1-7.20: EDUCAUSE.

Livingston, B. (2011) Harnessing Blogs for Learning, *T+D,* May 2011, pp76-77.

Lujan-Mora, S. & Juana-Espinosa, S. (2007) The use of weblogs in Higher Education: Benefits abd Barriers, Proceedings of the *International Technology, Education and Development (INTED),* Valencia, March 7-9 2007, pp1-7, IATED

Macduff, I. (2009) Using Blogs as a Teaching Tool in Negotiation, *Negotiation Journal,* January 2009, pp107-124

Richardson, W. (2010) Blogs, Wikis, Podcasts and other powerful web tools for classrooms, 3rd Edition, Thousand Oaks: Corwin.

Saunders, M., Lewis, P. & Thornhill, A. (2012) Research Methods for Business Students, 6th Edition, Pearson Education: England

Siemens, G. (2004) Connectivism: A Learning Theory for the Digital Age, [Online], http://itdl.org/journal/jan_05/article01.htm, [Accessed 25/05/12]

Verhagen, P. (2006) Connectivism: A new learning theory?, [Online], http://www.mendeley.com/research/connectivism-new-learning-theory-1/. [Accessed 25/05/12]

Yin, R (2009) Case Study Research – Design and Methods, 4th Edition, Sage Publications: USA.

"Digital Futures in Teacher Education": Exploring Open Approaches towards Digital Literacy

Anna Gruszczynska, Guy Merchant and Richard Pountney
Sheffield Hallam University, Sheffield, UK

Editorial Commentary
The storage, retrieval and multi-user dimension of Open Educational Resources has occasioned much debate in recent years and is influenced by our understanding of digital literacy. In offering a framework for digital literacy, this case study takes the discussion forward to position digital literacy as a set of socio-cultural and communicative practices. The particular value of this study is the way it puts young student voices centre stage in the debate; as teachers are forced further down the road of adoption of digital practices in their teaching, with often varied resources, training and support, Open Educational Resources were developed and trialled by student teachers in South Yorkshire in the UK and during the project all involved were encouraged to feedback and reflect critically on their use in relation to digital literacy practices. The two particular case studies presented here demonstrate some key issues in the technical versus the pedagogic nature of digital technologies.

Abstract: This paper reports the findings of a project "Digital Futures in Teacher Education" (DeFT) undertaken as part of the third phase of the Joint Information Systems Committee (JISC) UK Open Educational Resources (OER) programme. It builds on previous work (Gruszczynska and Pountney, 2012, 2013) that has addressed attempts to embed OER practice within the teacher education sector, and which has informed practice in teaching and learning in the school system involving digital literacy (Burnett and Merchant, 2011; Davies and Merchant, 2009). A framework for digital literacy is outlined, drawing heavily on socio-cultural models of digital practice (Merchant, 2011), that has the potential to re-imagine teachers and teaching, as well as learners and learning and which, at the same time, address the 'why' as well as the 'how' of digital literacy. This framework takes into account current debates (primarily within the UK but of relevance to European perspectives) focusing on issues of ICT, digital literacy and media literacy in the curriculum, which reflect a tension between digital literacy as a set of skills and competencies on the one hand and understandings that arise from socio-cultural and communicative practices on the other. Current understandings of digital literacy in the context of teacher education and OERs are explored and the potential for *digital literac(ies) for openness* is examined. This draws on data collected in the context of the DeFT project and includes meanings and perspectives on digital literacies as expressed by project participants. The effectiveness of a methodology that prizes reflexivity and participation is examined including a range of voices, including children's voices, in the meaning-making process and recommendations on the basis of the findings are made. In terms of a digital future for teacher education the paper highlights the need for practices, learning packages and tools to continue to evolve, in close cooperation with their potential users, and linked directly to classroom and schools as the site of this production.

Keywords: digital literacy, reflexivity, ICT curriculum, pedagogy, open educational resources

1. Introduction

The importance of new technologies in contemporary social, economic and cultural life has rapidly become an important theme in political debate, in policy development and in social science research. As social practices shape, and are shaped by the rapid diffusion of ever more sophisticated digital devices and applications, we are repeatedly presented with the opportunities and challenges of what have been described as a changing social order. This is a situation in which the communication economy is marked by new configurations of space and time, new levels of connectivity and interaction, and the global circulation of information. The shrinking gap between consumption and production, coupled with innovations in knowledge building and knowledge sharing, present exciting opportunities in many aspects of contemporary life (Warschauer and Matuchniak, 2010). Yet in the public imagination, technology is patterned by discourses of risk, surveillance, and rampant consumerism (Burnett and Merchant, 2011). Children and young people are often cast not only as the most active users of new technology, but also as those at most risk.

It is in this context that educators are challenged to respond to a multiplicity of issues, some of which end up being in direct conflict with one another. A well-worn example of this is the frequent call for them to give their students access to a wide range of popular web-sources, such as YouTube, which in the interest of a particular version of internet safety are repeatedly blocked by institutional firewalls (Davies and Merchant, 2009). But issues of overall purpose co-exist with such practical conundrums. Education systems, through curriculum policy and guidance, often encourage schools to develop quite specific and marketable skills that are intended to have economic traction. In contrast, some leading education theorists and researchers stress the importance of valuing and building upon children and young people's 'digital capital' – the practices and expertise that they already possess (Carrington and Robinson, 2009). Furthermore, in many Anglophone countries, the drive to develop competitive school systems through regimes of accountability and high stakes testing has led to a narrowing of curricular objectives. More often than not, these have fixed educators' attention and efforts on simple and measurable individual pupil achievement in 'core' areas such as literacy and numeracy in ways that are hard to reconcile with the digital practices referred to above.

The Digital Futures in Teacher Education (DeFT) project had to acknowledge these broad contextual factors whilst also addressing current debates on the role of Information and Communications Technology (ICT) in the curriculum and its relationship to digital literacies (Gruszczynska and Pountney 2012, 2013). As Merchant (2007) argues, there are a number of competing discourses in the UK that see ICT either as a set of skills (the National Curriculum for ICT, QCA 2000); as a tool or vehicle for learning (DfES, 2004) or as a transformative influence that has an impact on all aspects of schooling (DfES, 2005). These discourses are reflected most vividly in the recent Royal Society report (2012) that suggests that the current delivery of ICT in UK schools is highly unsatisfactory and uninspiring for the pupils, developing only basic skills while excluding the more advanced knowledge and understanding that could be gained through exposure of pupils to Computing Science (The Royal Society, 2012). Interestingly, in this context, digital literacy is defined as 'the general ability to use computers' alongside a set of skills such as the ability to use word processors or database software, with no reference to socio-cultural dimensions of digital literacies. The most recent development in this area, at the start of 2013, was consultation on the new curriculum for 'computing' following the disapplication of the programmes of study for ICT in 2012. In spite of these underlying tensions, the most interesting digital practices in the school sector have emerged from the work of enthusiastic innovators, often working alone, or in collaborative partnerships with researchers, or as part of informal grassroots networks such as 'teach meets'.

In England and Wales, the idea of a curriculum for technology lies in tatters, having been described by the Secretary of State for Education, Michael Gove, as 'flawed' and by others as 'off-putting' and 'dull' (Guardian Newspaper, 2012). In his address to the BETT (British Education and Training Technology) Conference, Gove underscored the political will to push digital literacy in schools, and proposed an 'open source curriculum' to encourage teachers' 'freedom and autonomy'. Alongside this rhetoric, there is recognition that digital literacy is applicable to all curriculum areas as well as in the more specialist domain of Computer Science. How these ideas will inform practice, in the wake of the Department for Education consultation process, remains to be seen. What is of broader interest here, is the way in which new technologies continue to unsettle traditional ways of thinking about curriculum and pedagogy and at the same time, appear to present exciting or radical possibilities for education (Merchant, 2009).

For new teachers, taking their first tentative steps into the complex arena of educational practice, there is very little guidance on technology. In England, and elsewhere, teacher preparation continues to be constrained by a regime of standards and accountability which more often than not mirrors that of the school sector (see above). For all the Information and Communications Technology (ICT) audits and sessions run by specialists, the teacher education curriculum is a narrow one. In addition to this, trainee teachers are likely to have a patchy experience of digital technology in the school context (Burnett, 2009) on account of variations in resource, access and classroom practice. Michael Gove promises to be 'looking at initial teacher training courses carefully in the coming year so that teachers get the skills and experience they need to use technology confidently' (Guardian Newspaper, 2012). We contribute to this debate by exploring how OERs can support teacher development in digital literacy (DL).

Debates about digital literacy have circulated since Gilster (1997) first coined the term. In a more recent development, JISC's framework looks at the 'anatomy' of digital literacy from two different but related perspectives. The first is as a frame for access, skills and practices. This includes the functional access to networks, devices, services, software and content that individuals require to exercise and develop digital literacy. The availability of these to individuals and social groups within society and in particular contexts such as education, is a key factor, especially in light of how, increasingly, the boundaries between work, leisure and education have become blurred. Here, the distinction between a practice and a skill is somewhat ill-defined and one in which media and information literacy are categorized alongside techno-social and academic practice. The second element of this anatomy is the contexts for these practices/skills, including the workplace, learning environments, the personal/social context and community. Key to this second frame is the concept of identity and its manifestation in social networks, lifestyles, learning and work communities (JISC, 2011). Inherent in this are two related sub-systems that are indicated by the labelling of this anatomy: ICT skills and Digital Practices.

A mapping of the DeFT project case studies to this framework highlights the value of this framework for the application of DL technologies to learning activities, but does not allow for the meanings that are made within and through these practices (Gillen and Barton, 2011). This latter view might serve to encourage teachers to engage with digital literacy throughout education, acknowledging, in so doing, how the skills and experience that learners (and their teachers) have or need is changing. Some commentators have argued for a baseline to identify those who are defined as digitally literate. However, it is our contention that this may not be helpful, given the proliferation of technologies each requiring different skills and operation. At the same time, the increasing possibilities offered by new technologies and the diversity of digital practices associated with them have prompted much debate around the growing gulf between literacy provision in schools and the rapidly changing digital literacies in learners' lives (Burnett, 2011, Beemt, van den et. al., 2011). Burnett brings up a number of arguments which attempt to account for this disconnect, such as inadequate access to equipment and competing pressures relating to print literacy. Another oft-cited argument is that pointing to an existence of a stark divide between teachers and pupils in terms of their competence and confidence levels, where the pupils are portrayed as 'digital natives' (Prensky, 2001), who have been exposed to new technologies from a very young age. However, a number of more recent studies critique this proposition and suggest a more nuanced understanding of divisions between individuals' experience of digital technologies, where levels of access and competence/confidence are determined by factors such as societal position, race, and gender, rather than age and educational status (Hargittai, 2010; Jones, 2013; Selwyn, 2004). A further body of research, involving a large scale investigation in Australian Schools, questions if a digital divide even exists or if stakeholders are overreacting (Bennett et al., 2008; Bennett and Maton, 2011).

2. Towards an open- source curriculum for teacher development – the role of OERs

As we have seen, there is a pressing need for teachers to engage with digital literacies throughout education, and increasingly the understandings and experiences that learners and their teachers have, and need, is changing as technology itself changes (Davies and Merchant, 2009). Open educational resources (OERs) are teaching and learning materials, freely available online for anyone to use, customise and add to, and as such, offer a powerful way of addressing this dynamic situation (Atkins et al., 2007). This paper arises in the context of the UK-wide Open Educational Resources programme, which took place between 2009 and 2012 and was a collaborative endeavour between the Higher Education Academy and Joint Information Systems Council (JISC), with funds provided by the Higher Education Funding Council for England (HEFCE). The authors of the paper adopt the definition of OERs offered in the context of the programme:

> ...teaching and learning materials (...) freely available online for everyone to use, whether you are an instructor, student or self-learner (...) [these] resources [are] contained in digital media collections from around the world (JISC/HEA 2010).

Of relevance to this paper is a broadened definition of OERs, proposed by Mackintosh (2011), which identifies three interrelated dimensions: educational values (i.e. barrier-free access to the resources), pedagogical utility (anyone accessing OERs should be able to reuse, revise, remix and redistribute the resources) and technology enablers (i.e. OERs should be in a format that ensures that they are 'meaningfully' editable). This means that potential (re-)users of OERs are positioned not as mere consumers but as active participants in the process of creating and sharing the resources (Tosato and Bodi, 2012). Whilst there have been three phases of OER funding for Higher Education to date, there remains little coordinated development of resources for the UK school sector. A notable exception has been the work of the British Educational Communications and Technology Agency (BECTA). The BECTA-funded project 'Repurpose, Create, Share' aimed to create and share digital resources across participating secondary schools and the National Education Network (Hemsley, 2008).

In terms of issues of relevance to the school sector, most existing research focuses on the implementation of OERs in developing countries. This includes initiatives such as the High School BLOSSOMS (Blended Learning Open Source Science or Math Studies Initiative) project in the Middle East Region (Larson and Murray, 2008) which examined low-tech solutions to overcoming barriers to accessing OERs. Similarly the Teacher Education in Sub-Saharan Africa project (TESSA) undertaken by Open University examined issues involved in supporting user communities to harness and integrate OERs for their own systems and cultures (Thakrar et al., 2009; Wolfenden, et al. 2010, Murphy and Wolfenden 2012). In a European context there is a strong recognition of the need to meet the professional development needs of teachers:

The teaching professions now face rapidly changing demands, which require a new set of competences....The growing availability of online content and open educational resources provides new opportunities to pupils and students, but also to teaching professions (EC, 2012:6).

Furthermore, it is evident that the implications of the increasing use of technology for learning, including the need for a level of competency that makes the use of technology for learning possible has the potential to foster inequalities of access and opportunity. The EU Key Competence Framework (Europa, 2010) supports this view stating "... *transversal skills will be valued more than the specific bodies of knowledge that schools have traditionally taught"*. This paper questions whether these transversal skills are yet to be addressed by current conceptions of digital competence; that these conceptions are provoked by an impulse to consume technology and not necessarily to apply it; and that these conceptions are reinforced by a narrow view of the use of tools for learning and teaching. Together these restrictions have a multiplier effect on practice that if not addressed can continue to limit the potential for 'digital competence as a human right' (Ferrari, 2012) in which the possibilities for teachers are closed before they can be captured in their imaginations.

In the UK context, OERs could make a significant contribution to work on digital literacies in teacher development. There are two reasons for this. Firstly, in the UK, as elsewhere, there is a diversity of models of teacher preparation, including university-school partnerships and programmes that are entirely school based. This means that trainee teachers, or for that matter early career teachers, are likely to need access to support materials at different stages in their preparation for teaching and at a variety of points during their academic or professional study. The flexibility offered by OERs fits well with this diversity of provision. Secondly, the field of digital literacy itself is characterised by its fluidity as new devices become available and new programmes and applications are developed. The rapid changes in the curriculum structures of compulsory schooling (see above) increase this sense of fluidity. We suggest that the adaptability and reusability of OERs has considerable potential in this complex situation and might contribute to an open source curriculum for teacher development.

One outcome of this is a reliance on a facility with technology that the authors of this paper broadly describe as *digital literac(ies) for openness*. This approach extends the notion that OERs possess a pedagogical utility (Mackintosh, 2011) to examine the landscape in which teacher identities are being constructed, socio-culturally and socio-politically as part of a pedagogic discourse (Bernstein, 1990). Teachers' responses to the pedagogical potential of technology are seen to be shaped by a regulative discourse (ibid.) and by complex models of compliance and autonomy (Pountney, 2003) that may not necessarily result in practice that might be termed innovative (Merchant, 2005). The inclusion of open educational resources for learning and teaching within teacher education programmes to date, for example, is primarily focussed on finding and using resources rather than modifying and creating new ones. This emphasis on 'make and mend' arises partly from the reality of busy teachers' lives and can limit the potential to move beyond the simplistic 'goals to means' paradigm that tends to dominate technology use in schools (Underwood and Dillon, 2011). Accordingly, a view emerges of teachers' work as 'bricolage' (Hatton, 1989) - as the ad hoc material manipulation of resources and the 'craft' in the use of 'whatever is to hand' (Levi-Strauss, 1974: 17). Teachers' capacity to move beyond this positioning of their role as *'bricoleurs'* relies to an extent on their agency to imagine pedagogy and the curriculum: how they might become, or aspire to being, *'designers'*, perhaps. The implications of this for teacher education are explored in the following sections of this paper and are illustrated from the DeFT project case studies.

3. The project and its findings

The DeFT project team, based at Sheffield Hallam University and the University of Sheffield, designed OERs, in the form of an Open Textbook (Connexions, 2009), to address the opportunities and challenges of creative and innovative uses of digital literacy in the school and teacher education sectors. The team worked with teachers in primary and secondary schools in South Yorkshire to develop case studies of digital practices in schools - practices which included the use of mobile devices, digital video, Web2.0 applications, and school intranets. Course tutors and teacher education students were involved in trialling and developing the OERs which comprise resources that support effective practice with digital literacy for teachers at all stages of their careers.

The two key outputs of the project, released under Creative Commons licence, were:

1. The Open textbook (see Figure 1 for screenshot of homepage)- an Open Resource on Digital Literacy for Educators, Teachers and Schools which explores the challenges of involving learners with digital literacies; incorporating the two core elements: digital literacies in the context of professional development and digital literacies for creative learners. The OT comprises 100,000 words arranged in 6 chapters and contains 2 'alternative' tables of contents: 1) Key Questions; and 2) Digital Literacy for Teachers. It also has a unique Thinking Space function that allows users to 'like', 'tag', 'annotate' and 'export' content to a personalised open textbook (under development). (see www.digitalfutures.org)

2. Digital Bloom - in the DeFT project Digital Bloom became a focus for exploring the intersections of digital literacy and creativity. Participants were encouraged to reflect on the relationship between creativity and learners' digital literacy practice, both inside and outside formal education institutions. The central metaphor for these activities was 'Digital Bloom': an abstract concept represented by a field of flowers (see Figure 2), where each flower reflects an individual understanding of digital literacy and the field symbolises the social layer (see the case study below). In this public meadow the project team and partners reflected on digital literacy. The Digital Bloom application has been used by several schools in 'private' meadows (see www.digitalbloom.org).

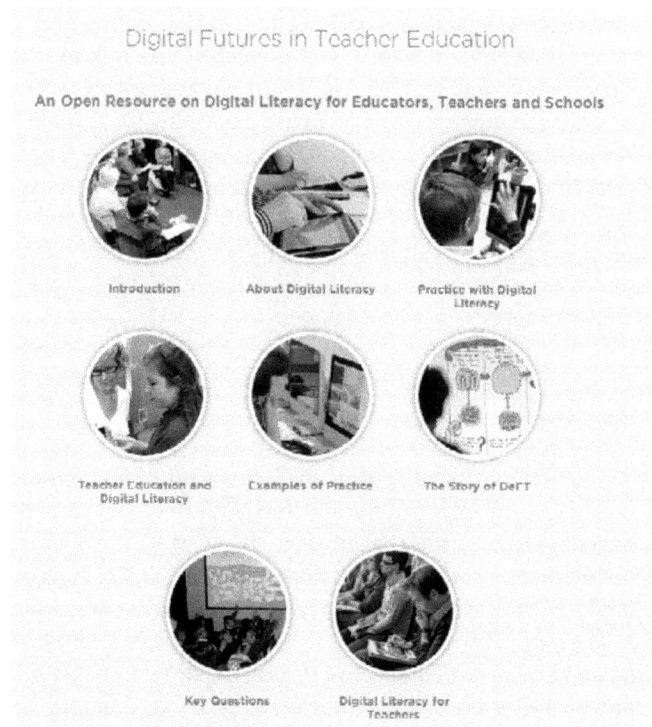

Figure 1. Screenshot of the Open Textbook hopemage

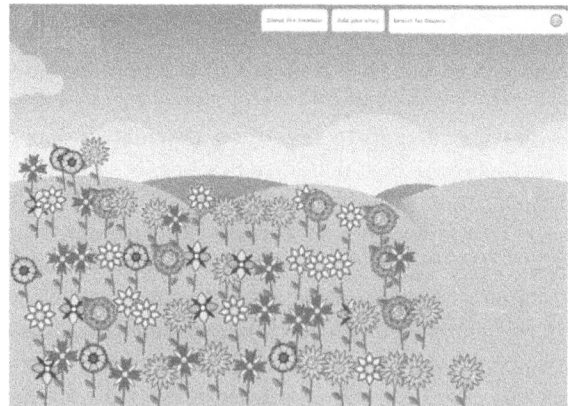

Figure 2. Digital Bloom meadow

The emphasis of this project on practice - and in particular digital practices and social aspects of digital literacy - was realised through a methodology that aimed to enrich practice by empowering teachers and teacher educators to reflect and critically engage with their own practice and their own communities, wherever appropriate. This heightened the potential for the exchange and development of practice and expertise through the system of the open textbook resource and learning package. With regard to teacher competences this project addressed first order (teaching) skills, and second order (teaching about teaching) skills. One key outcome was the preparation of new teacher training courses in digital literacy and the use of OER for learning and teaching in formal and informal settings.

An important part of the DeFT project methodology was to involve teachers and students, trainee teachers and university colleagues as equal partners in exploring the possibilities of digital literacy. This produced a temporary learning community that in itself provides a useful model for developing practice in this area (Davies & Merchant, forthcoming). To achieve this we adopted a reflexive approach (see also Gruszczynska, 2012), which informed the project methodology. A guiding principle, therefore, was that through structured reflection, teaching practices can be critically reviewed and hence better understood. This helped in articulating approaches to digital literacies which mapped onto the experiences of project participants. In terms of practical realisation of that approach, all project participants (core team, teachers, course tutors and students) contributed to a series of reflexive tasks in which they responded to prompts provided by the project team at five points in the project lifecycle. These prompts varied slightly for each of the groups in acknowledgement of their particular working context. Participants were encouraged to offer their responses in a variety of formats such as text, audio or video, depending on personal preferences. The reflections then informed the development of the Open Textbook and became its integral part. One of the clear messages coming out of the reflections is that the subject of digital literacy, although not new, needed to be unpacked and scrutinized in the context of education. The enthusiasm that the project engendered in those who took part is remarkable, and the reflections demonstrate that the project has broadened and supported new perceptions of digital technologies.

The responses were collated to identify emerging themes and to gain a sense of developing understandings of digital literacy. A digest of these reflections was shared amongst participants shortly after each stage, thus contributing to a cumulative sense of meanings generated by the group. The emphasis on reflexive tasks draws on a body of research on teacher inquiry teaching (Cochran-Smith and Lytle, 1993) in which teachers research their own practice, generating new knowledge by identifying and responding to dissonances within their practice (Timperley et al., 2007). This enrichment approach became an integral part of the school-based work of the project. Here the project team and participating teachers constructed case studies of their work. Teachers in 10 different schools were involved in this phase and worked in different contexts (from the early years through to secondary/high school) with students from a range of socio-economic and cultural backgrounds. In the following section, we examined the meanings and perspectives on digital literacies as expressed by teachers in two of the participating schools through their classroom work and their reflections. In recognition of the methodological difficulties of generalising from case study research (Lincoln and Guba, 1984), we have simply chosen 2 examples to illustrate the range of the work undertaken.

4. Developing digital literacy in the context of schools and teacher education

Case study data were archived on a project wiki and included notes from school visits, interactions between researchers and teachers at project meetings, as well as supporting material from blogs and reflexive tasks. During the lifetime of the project, the wiki was password protected; it was openly released as one of the outputs of the project and is now available from deftoer3.pbworks.com; this was consistent with our approach, based on engagement with openness and reflexivity.

Here, we use this case study material to illustrate tensions and understandings of digital literacy in practice. For ethical reasons fictitious names have been used for both schools and teachers in the accounts. The first case study depicts the work undertaken by a primary school teacher and her Year 2 class (6-7 year olds) at Mondrian Primary School in Sheffield. The second case study is based around the work of an English and Media Studies teacher working at the Warhol School in Rotherham (9-16 year olds).

The work in Mondrian Primary School focused on the use of the iPad 'Brushes' app, and emerged from project collaboration with Sheffield Children's Festival – a local cultural event which celebrates the creativity of local children. As part of this work, the children participated in an artist-led workshop in which they drew digital flowers using the Brushes app. The flowers were then incorporated into a mural developed by a graphic designer. Following the workshop, children were invited to offer their comments via the class blog, where the project team members asked them questions about their experience. The teacher leading on this case study also offered her reflections on the process through participation in project reflexive task (see above). Her comments emphasise children's confidence with technology and the speed with which the children picked up the basic principles of using the mobile devices and the app:

> *Children as young as 4 in reception were using them [i.e. iPads] with ease, moving between apps and the home screen quickly and without concern for the equipment itself. They were confident and surprisingly competent. When I sat down and showed them how to use the app, I went through it all, then handed them over. It wasn't until 5 mins in when I realised I'd forgotten to tell them how to turn them on…. It was then that I realised they really didn't need me at all!*

In this account, the children are positioned as self-reliant, and there is little perceived need for teacher intervention. This teacher then subsequently added, that on the basis of this pre-workshop trial, she decided to amend the lesson plan for the workshop so that it no longer included a basic introduction to using iPads preferring instead to allow children to start using 'Brushes' straight away.

Figure 3. An example of an i-Pad flower drawn by children at Mondrian

In this particular case, the children had access to iPads in the classroom for about two weeks and some of them could also use them at home. Most of the children when they talked about the work focused their enjoyment of the workshop. For instance one child commented *'I loved having a go on the iPads it was so much fun I can't wait to go on them again'*, with another adding that they loved the experience *'because they [i.e.] iPads are cool'*. Other children were similarly enthusiastic and described the iPads as *'APSULUTE AMAZING!!!'* (original spelling) and 'magical'. In this way the children's comments emphasised the playful nature of the experience (Robinson and Willet, 2008) and a certain level of fascination with the technology, in referring to the iPads as *'magical'*. On a related note, when the teacher offered her account of the workshop, she commented being surprised by how focused the children were throughout the session and that for the entire hour you could *'hear a pin drop'*, which was usually not the case during other art classes! In this account, the technology becomes a transparent medium which offers a chance for the children to engage in an activity which is so enjoyable that they maintain high levels of focus effortlessly. A similar approach to digital literacy is illustrated through the case study of work at Warhol School which focused on the use of digital video for enhancing pupil communication and critical thinking skills.

The second case study offers an insight into the understandings of digital literacies and openness in the context of teacher training where a tutor on the Post Graduate Certificate in Education (PGCE) course at one of participating universities, invited her students to reflect on digital-literacy issues within their practice, and engaged them in a discussion on digital literacy and OER issues. The key element of the work was based on student participation in a reflexive exercise where they were asked questions aimed to elicit their perceptions of digital literacy and OERs.

The first question focused on understandings of digital literacy in a professional context. For the most part, the students subscribed to a definition of literacy that focused on skills, for example being able to use a variety of technologies in a competent manner. They also commented on the ways in which the PGCE course gave them a better understanding of how they might embed digital practices in their teaching to make the classroom environment more engaging and inclusive. While they reported mainly positive experiences from placements, they also mentioned frustrations related to inconsistent access to software and hardware.

The second question addressed student attitudes to sharing resources online and with their peers and/or pupils. Most students indicated that they were indeed sharing their teaching materials:

> *I have shared my resources with my course mates in a Facebook group. I have also shared them with the department at my placement school (on the MLE). I did this because I use others' resources so I think it is fair to share myself.*

Others elaborated on the benefits of sharing for professional practice, arguing that it stimulated good teaching:

A teacher who shares is an efficient and reflective teacher – by sharing you are not reinventing the wheel but constantly improving it.

I think sharing good practice is a good part of developing professionally and using tried and tested resources – adapting them, differentiating them, reinventing them – saves time and often improves the quality of learning for students when I have run out of creative ideas!

While students were happy to share resources within their immediate network – peers on the course, teachers on placements – they had a number of reservations when it came to releasing their resources openly online and sharing them with a potentially unknown audience:

I am always willing to share my resources with other members of staff in school and have done this on a regular basis at my current placement. I have shied away from sharing materials online contexts, however, as I always feel a little protective of the things I produce because I invest a lot of time in making resources, and don't feel entirely comfortable at present to make it freely available for anyone to download. (I like knowing who is using it!)

Others mentioned concerns about receiving negative feedback and the time investment needed to upload resources online, with a small minority concerned about pedagogical issues and the potential risk of stifling creativity through excessive reliance on resources 'off the shelf':

These data revealed issues relevant to the embedding of OERs in the context of teacher education. Importantly, within the group there was little awareness of the term itself, despite ample evidence of a well-developed culture of sharing. At the same time, while trainee teachers seemed keen to share their resources online with their immediate network, they were much more reluctant to share beyond the circle of people they know and, for instance, release the materials openly to educational repositories. For the most part, they cited fear of negative feedback to explain their reluctance; some also commented on perceived lack of control once resources were shared more widely. It is therefore crucial to raise awareness among trainee teachers and their educators about OERs, to dispel misconceptions and also to demonstrate how resources could be shared to maximise the benefits for producers and consumers. By releasing teaching resources into a well-respected educational repository, teachers could receive professional recognition from a wider community of practice and useful feedback, which could in turn, help to improve their practice and continue gaining valuable competencies in the area of digital literacy for openness, identified as a crucial future key competence by the authors of this paper. As indicated previously, there is a pressing need for teachers to engage with digital literacy throughout education, and increasingly the skills and experience that learners (and their teachers) have or need is changing (Davies and Merchant, 2009). At the same time, new teachers to the profession, in all subject areas, are increasingly expected to have access to and become adept users of digital technology.

The accounts of many of the project participants reflect the tension between understandings of digital literacy as a technical competence, and a communicative practice. Conceptualising digital literacy as a technical skill was often seen as reductive and potentially problematic, particularly since this approach did not allow for exploring the creative possibilities offered by technology. For instance, during the first project meeting, one of the PGCE (Postgraduate Certificate in Education) tutors involved with the project expressed his concern about the amount of time that often needs to be spent on instrumental aspects of technology before there is space for more creative approaches, adding that at times educators 'fetishise technology when a piece of pen and paper will work just as well'. At the same meeting, a teacher pointed out that technological mastery tended to reduce learning with technology to operational skill rather than application, and that this did not translate well into sophisticated uses of tools at the disposal of learners:

What do you think a child does when you give them an iPad? Watch what they do: they get the camera, take a picture of themselves (...) they will do that for hours and hours and hours. Now where's the digital literacy in that?'

Furthermore, emphasizing technical issues to the exclusion of authentic uses of digital literacy meant that the debates often focused on barriers and limitations, rather than enablers. In this sense understanding of digital literacy as a skill set was quite disempowering for teachers who worried about their own competence levels and felt relatively de-skilled in comparison to their pupils. Overall, the project participants were keen to move away from a reductive approach and adopt a more sophisticated one which favoured understandings of digital literacy embedded within socio-cultural practices. For instance, when talking about the rationale to embed digital literacy within their teaching practice, the student teachers suggested that:

[I]t is important to amalgamate ideas related to digital literacy into lessons, it makes sense in the context of 'the way everything is heading'; the world is moving on, (...) it is best that the kids are informed and understand when they are being manipulated by Facebook etc. This way, if they are properly informed, they can get the best out of the tools they are using

This approach highlights raising the awareness of learners to be able to appreciate and negotiate the complex landscape of digital technologies (Burnett and Merchant, 2011) and to move from being passive consumers of technology to becoming more active and empowered consumers/ producers (Bruns, 2008). Thus, the above quotes illustrate the multi-faceted aspects of digital literacies and the process of meaning-making where project participants are constantly re-evaluating their understandings of digital literacy both for themselves and others involved in the project.

A number of key issues emerge from these data and underscore some current themes in the field. These could be summarised in the form of the following recommendations for exploring the potential of digital literacy in teaching and learning. Digital literacy:

- offers alternative ways of representing, ideas and experiences, and this is attractive to educators when it allows for ways of capitalising on student learning within (and across) the curriculum
- can promote high levels of student engagement and enjoyment. This often includes playful approaches which are seen as highly motivating
- often seems to present children and young people as experts, either because it draws on their existing experience, or because they are thought to be quick to adapt to new technologies
- has both technical and expressive dimensions. The relationship between these dimensions is contentious both from ideological and pedagogical perspectives
-

5. Discussion

In a relatively short length of time, ways of thinking about digital technologies in schools seem to have shifted in the UK. When the Deft project began in September 2011, it was pretty clear that the ICT curriculum was the last place to look for interesting digital practices. But as the academic year has unfolded, competing conceptualizations of digital literacy surfaced. Using literacy as a shorthand for the kinds of knowledge and competences that are applied for making meanings in the real world shifts the focus to the outcome of an educative process (formal or informal) in which literacy is 'the knowledge and skills learners acquire' (Buckingham 2003: 4) that are bundled together (Livingstone 2005). This has implications for the sociocultural understandings associated with the term literacy and is contextually bound with the discussions and cases of practice in this paper.

Some of these are not too far away from the ideas first put forward by Gilster (1997:290) who suggested that DL is:

'a set of skills to access the Internet; find, manage and edit digital information; join in communications; and otherwise en-

gage with an online information and communication network. In simple terms, digital literacy is the ability to properly use and evaluate digital resources, tools and services and apply it to their lifelong learning process.' (Gilster, 1997:220).

Yet, current work in fields such as literacy studies, media, popular culture and information studies continues to offer rich and competing views of what is central to an understanding of digital literacy. Alongside this, the relatively young field of educational technology itself is informed by a range of disciplines and knowledge domains (Czerniewicz, 2010) in which education professionals and scholars are faced with a range of perspectives in which concepts, terms and relations and research procedures are ill-defined (Alexander et al, 2006). This explains, to some extent, the sheer diversity of existing accounts of digital literacy (Lankshear and Knobel, 2010) and highlights the difficulty in addressing this in teacher education. In the context of the DeFT project, our engagement with the case study material has focused on a socio-cultural perspective: 'the constantly changing practices through which people make traceable meanings using digital technologies' (Gillen and Barton, 2010:9).

In the project schools, work was not exclusively driven by digital technology, but of course it always contained that element. More often than not, it was embedded within wider formal and non-formal learning. From this point of view, digital communication played a part in a wide variety of different kinds of learning - in classrooms and outside of classrooms; in art projects; in community projects; writing projects; and in English and media projects. These interpretations of digital literacy move us away from thinking about an ICT curriculum, since what we have seen is a widespread interest in exploring the 'digital in the curriculum' - the sorts of practices that might work, and the kinds of barriers that might need to be overcome.

The project has identified digital practices and ICT skills as a problem space in which accounts of digital literacy and the (re-)use of open resources are incomplete or only partially realised in school contexts. With the advance of technology new issues concerning access, publication and ownership of open educational resources are emerging.

The process of developing an Open Textbook on Digital Literacy for Teachers (see http://www.digitalfutures.org), in itself an OER, has exemplified these issues. While 'openness' covers a range of concepts in relation to teaching and learning practices we aim to make a clearer connection between OERs and digital literacy and offer ways of exploring this further. In terms of a digital future for teacher education it is important that practices continue to evolve in which learning packages and tools are developed in close cooperation with their potential users and that are linked directly to classroom and schools as the site of this production. Within this is the need to re-examine digital literac(ies) for openness in the context of the debate around technology in pedagogy and in the curriculum in order that a better understanding of what is emerging (or shifting) can be achieved.

References

Alexander S., Harper C., Anderson T.D., Golja T., Lowe D., McLaughlan R., Schaverien L. and Thompson D. (2006) Towards a mapping of the field of e-learning. In *Edmedia World Conference on Educational Multimedia, Hypermedia and Telecommunications* Pearson, E. and P. Bohrman (eds.) Association for the Advancement of Computing in Education (pp1636–1642), Orlando.

Atkins D.E., Brown J.S. and Hammond A.L. (2007). "A Review of the Open Educational Resources (OER) Movement: Achievements, Challenges, and New Opportunities", Hewlett Foundation. [online] http://www.oerderves.org/wp-content/uploads/2007/03/a-review-of-the-open-educational-resources-oer-movement_final.pdf (Last accessed 22 February 2013).

Beemt, A. van den, S. Akkerman and P.R.J. Simons (2011). "Patterns of interactive media use among contemporary youth." Journal of Computer Assisted Learning, Vol. 27, No.2, pp103–118.

Bennett, S. and Maton, K. (2011) Intellectual field or faith-based religion: Moving on from the idea of 'digital natives', in Thomas, M. (ed.) *Deconstructing Digital Natives: Young people, technology and the new literacies* (pp169-185), Routledge: New York.

Bennett, S, Maton, K, and Kervin, L. (2008). "The 'digital natives" debate: A critical review of evidence." British Journal of Educational Technology, Vol. 39, No. 5, pp775–786.

Bernstein, B. (1990) *The structuring of pedagogic discourse*. Routledge: London.

Bruns, A. (2008) Blogs, Wikipedia, Second Life, and Beyond: From Production to Produsage. Peter Lang: New York.

Buckingham, D. (2003). Media education: literacy, learning and contemporary culture. Polity: Cambridge.

Burnett, C. (2011). "Pre-service teachers' digital literacy practices: exploring contingency in identity and digital literacy in and out of educational contexts" Language and Education, Vol 25, No.5, pp433-459.

Burnett, C. (2009) "Personal digital literacies versus classroom literacies: investigating pre-service teachers' digital lives in and beyond the classroom". In: V. Carrington and M. Robinson. (Eds.) *Digital Literacies: social learning and classroom practices* (pp115-129), Sage: London.

Burnett, C. and Merchant, G. (2011) "Is there a space for critical literacy in the context of new media?" English, Practice and Critique, Vol 10, No. 1, pp41-57.

Carrington, V. and Robinson. M.(2009) (eds.) *Digital Literacies: Social Learning and Classroom Practice*. Sage: London.

Cochran-Smith, M. and Lytle, S. (1993) *Inside/outside: Teachers, research, and knowledge*. Teachers College Press: New York.

Connexions (2009). "What are open textbooks?" [online] http://cnx.org/content/m15226/latest/ (Last accessed 2 March 2013).

Czerniewicz, L. 2010. "Educational technology – Mapping the terrain with Bernstein as cartographer", Journal of Computer Assisted Learning, Vol 26, No. 6, pp523–34.

Davies, J. & Merchant, G. (forthcoming) "Digital Literacy and Teacher Education", In P.Benson & A. Chik *Popular Culture, Pedagogy and Teacher Education: International Perspectives* Routledge: London.

Davies, J. and Merchant, G. (2009) *Web 2.0 for Schools: Social Participation and Learning*. Peter Lang: New York.

DfES. (2004). Learning and Teaching using ICT: example materials from Foundation Stage to Year 6. DfES: London.

DfES. (2005). Harnessing Technology: Transforming Learning and Children's Services. DfES: London.

Europa (2010) "Key competences for lifelong learning", [online] http://europa.eu/legislation_summaries/education_training_youth/lifelong_learning/c11090_en.htm (Last accessed 28 February 2013)

European Commission [EC](2012) "Supporting the Teaching Professions for Better Learning Outcomes", [online] http://ec.europa.eu/education/news/rethinking/sw374_en.pdf (Last accessed 28 February 2013)

Ferrari, A. (2012). "Digital competence in practice: an analysis of frameworks" JRC Technical

Reports. [online] http://ftp.jrc.es/EURdoc/JRC68116.pdf (Last accessed 1 March 2013).
Gillen, J. and Barton, D. (2011). Digital literacies. A research briefing by the technology enhanced learning phase of the teaching and learning research programme. London Knowledge Lab, Institute of Education: London.
Gilster, P. (1997) *Digital Literacy*. John Wiley: New York.
Gruszczynska, A (2012). "The value of reflexive methods for enhancing pedagogical practice in the context of OER development", Higher Education Academy: York [online] http://www.heacademy.ac.uk/assets/documents/oer/OER_CS_Anna_Gruszczynska_Value_of_Reflective_Methods.pdf (Last accessed 1 March 2013).
Gruszczynska, A and Pountney, R. (2013) "Developing the concept of Digital Literacy in the context of Schools and Teacher Education", Enhancing Learning in the Social Sciences, Vol 5, No.1 (in press)
Gruszczynska, A and Pountney, R. (2012). "Digital Futures in Teacher Education: Exploring the opportunities and challenges of creative uses of digital literacy in schools" In: *Proceedings of OpenCourseWare Consortium Global 2012: Celebrating 10 Years of OpenCourseWare*. Cambridge, MA. [online] http://www.ucel.ac.uk/oer12/papers/227%20Digital%20Futures%20in%20Teacher%20Education%20-%20Anna%20Gruszczynska.doc (Last accessed 2 March 2013)
Guardian Newspaper (2012) "Text of Michael Gove's BETT conference address, January 12th, 2012", [online] http://www.guardian.co.uk/education/2012/jan/11/digital-literacy-michael-gove-speech (Last accessed 18 February 2013)
Hargittai, E. (2010). "Digital Na(t)ives? Variation in Internet Skills and Uses among Members of the 'Net Generation'", Sociological Inquiry, Vol 80, No. 1, pp92-113.
Hemsley, K. (2008). Becta 'Repurpose, Create, Share' in the YHGfL Region. Unpublished project report.
Joint Information Systems Committee (JISC). (2011). "Digital literacy anatomised: access, skills and practices", [online] http://jiscdesignstudio.pbworks.com/w/file/40474828/Digital%20literacies%20anatomy.pdf (Last accessed 21 February 2013).
Joint Information Systems Committee (JISC)/ Higher Education Academy (HEA). (2010). "What are Open Educational Resources?" [online] https://openeducationalresources.pbworks.com/w/page/24836860/What%20are%20Open%20Educational%20Resources (Last accessed 19 February 2013).

Jones, C. (2013). "The new shape of the student" In Reshaping Learning (pp91-112). Springer Berlin Heidelberg. Lankshear, C. and Knobel, M. (2010) *New Literacies: Everyday Practices and Social Learning* (3rd Edition). Open University Press: Maidenhead

Lankshear, C. and Knobel, M. (2010) *New Literacies: Everyday Practices and Social Learning* (3rd Edition). Open University Press: Maidenhead.

Larson, R. C., and Murray, E. (2008). "Open educational resources for blended learning in high schools: Overcoming impediments in developing countries", Journal of Asynchronous Learning Networks, Vol 12, No. 1, pp85-103.

Levi-Strauss, C. (1974) *The Savage Mind* (2d edition), Weidenfeld and Nicholson: London.

Lincoln, Y. and Guba, G. (1984) *Naturalistic Inquiry*. Sage: Beverley Hills, CA.

Livingstone, S. (2005). *Media literacy – challenges ahead*. (Westminster Media Forum, Implementing Media Literacy: Empowerment, Participation and Responsibility), LSE: London.

Mackintosh, W. (2011). "OERU Planning meeting: Information pack", [online] http://wikieducator.org/index.php?oldid=659570 (Last accessed 12 February 2013).

Merchant, G. (2011) "Critical media literacy", In C.A.Chapelle (ed), *The Encyclopedia of Applied Linguistics*. Wiley-Blackwell: Oxford.

Merchant, G. (2005). "Digikids: cool dudes and the new writing", E-Learning, Vol 2, No. 1, pp50-60.

Merchant, G. (2007) "Writing the future in the digital age", Literacy. Vol 41, No. 3, pp118-128.

OECD (2010) "Teachers' Professional Development: Europe in international comparison", Paris, OECD. [online] http://ec.europa.eu/education/school-education/doc/talis/report_en.pdf (Last accessed 28 January 2013)

QCA (2000). Information and Communication Technology, the National Curriculum for England. Qualifications and Curriculum Authority: London.

Murphy, P. and Wolfenden, F. (2013) "Developing a pedagogy of mutuality in a capability approach – Teachers' experiences of using the open educational resources (OER) of the teacher education in sub-Saharan Africa (TESSA) programme" (in press) *International Journal of Educational Development,* [online] http://dx.doi.org/doi:10.1016/j.ijedudev.2012.09.010 (Last accessed 11 February 2013).

Pountney, R. (2003). "Ready and willing? Factors impacting on engagement with professional development in ICT in primary schools", Paper presented at the ITTE (The Association for Information Technology in Teacher Education) 2003 conference, Leeds, July 2003.

Prensky, M. (2001). "Digital natives, digital immigrants", On the Horizon, Vol 9, No. 5, pp1–6.
Robinson, M. and R. Willett (Eds) (2008). *Play, Creativity and digital cultures*. Routledge: London.
The Royal Society. (2012). *Shut down or restart? The way forward for computing in UK schools*. London: The Royal Society. [online] http://royalsociety.org/uploadedFiles/Royal_Society_Content/education/policy/computing-in-schools/2012-01-12-Computing-in-Schools.pdf (Last accessed 28 February 2013).
Selwyn, N. (2004). "Reconsidering political and popular understandings of the digital divide" *New Media Society*, Vol 6, No. 3, pp341–62.
Thakrar, J., Zinn, D., and Wolfenden, F. (2009). "Harnessing open educational resources to the challenges of teacher education in Sub-Saharan Africa", International review of research in open and distance learning, Vol 10, No. 4, [online] www.irrodl.org/index.php/irrodl/article/download/705/1342 (Last accessed 28 February 2013).
Timperley, H., Wilson, A., Barrar, H. and Fung, I. (2007). *Teacher Professional Learning and Development: Best Evidence Synthesis Iteration*. Ministry of Education: Wellington, New Zealand.
Tosato,P. and Bodi, G. (2011). "Collaborative Environments to Foster Creativity, Reuse and Sharing of OER" *European Journal of Open, Distance and E-Learning. Special Themed Issue on Creativity and Open Educational Resources (OER)*. [online] http://www.eurodl.org/materials/special/2011/Tosato_Bodi.pdf (Last accessed 11 February 2013).
Warschauer, M. and Matuchniak, T. (2010) "New Technology and Digital Worlds: Analyzing Evidence of Equity in Access, Use, and Outcomes", Review of Research in Education, Vol 34, No.1, pp.179-225.
Wolfenden, F.; Umar, A.; Aguti, J. and Abdel Gafar, A. (2010). "Using OERs to improve teacher quality: emerging findings from TESSA", Paper presented at the *Sixth Pan Commonwealth Forum on Open Learning*, 24-28 Nov 2010, Kochi, India. [online] http://oro.open.ac.uk/27174/2/PCF_6_Full_paper_Wolfenden_Amended.pdf (Last accessed 19 February 2013).

The Yin/Yang of Innovative Technology Enhanced Assessment for Promoting Student Learning

Maggie Hutchings, Anne Quinney, Kate Galvin and Vince Clark
Bournemouth University, Bournemouth, UK

Editorial Commentary
Nowhere is there more challenge yet also potential for technology enhancement of learning than in very large cohorts of students in Higher Education. So much of what we read today about the use of digital learning technologies works simply for small to medium sized groups of students, but when transferred to a cohort of 600 on a physical campus, the personalisation, and very flexibility of learning technologies can lead to complex logistical challenges, particularly for assessment practice. This is the focus of this case study, which takes seriously the need for assessment for rather than of learning, and contrasts front-loaded formalised multiple choice question testing with instant feedback and scoring and the assessment of reflective blogs which can offer potentially deeper learning engagement and will require considerable staff resource after rather than before submission. The case offers student feedback on these types of assessment and commentary on the use of audience-response surveys in class as a formative assessment method used to help with exam preparation.

Abstract: While more sophisticated and constructively aligned assessment is encouraged to promote higher level learning, it is easier to assess knowledge and comprehension than critical thinking and making judgements (Bryan & Clegg 2006). Managing the logistics and resources required for assessing large numbers of students challenges the ethos of placing students at the heart of the learning process and helping them take responsibility for their own learning. The introduction of innovative technology enhanced assessment strategies contests our understanding of the purposes of assessment and affords opportunities for more integrated and personalised approaches to learning and assessment across disciplines. This paper will examine the design, implementation and impacts of innovative assessment strategies forming an integral part of a collaborative lifeworld-led transprofessional curriculum delivered to cohorts of 600 students in health and social work using technology to connect learners to wide-ranging, humanising perspectives on evidence for guiding practice. Innovative assessment technologies included group blogs, multiple choice electronic or computer assisted assessment (CAA), and an audience response system (ARS) affording combinations of assessment for learning and assessment of learning. We will explore, through analyses of student assessment experiences and student and staff evaluations, how these innovative assessment approaches contribute to effective and efficient blended education enabling students to enhance their practice through promoting and developing critical thinking and reflection for judgement-based practice (Polkinghorne 2004). Secondly, we will debate the yin and yang of contrasting and connecting values associated with the controlled, systematic measurement and objectivity of multiple choice assessments, compared with the formative, iterative and subjective nature of reflective blogging. We will consider relationships between teaching and learning strategies and experiences, breadth and depth of knowledge, passive and active approaches to learning, efficiency and effectiveness, individual and group, multiple choice and discursive assessments, face-to-face and online, on-campus and off-campus learning and assessment experiences.

Keywords: innovative assessment; computer assisted assessment; technology enhanced learning; group blogs; audience response systems

1. Introduction: Innovative technology-enhanced assessment

For assessment to be considered innovative it needs to do much more than introduce new technologies into the assessment diet for students. Innovative assessment strategies need to encourage assessment *for* learning over assessment *of* learning. Bryan and Clegg (2006) argue that innovative assessment should enable student learning and judgements, rather than acting as instruments of justification, measurement and limitation. But introducing innovative assessment can be a high-stake investment fraught with risk for students and higher education institutions (HEIs). The significance of assessment for students cannot be underestimated. Assessment frames learning by creating learning activities which orientate learning behaviour (Gibbs in Bryan & Clegg 2006) and while students can escape bad teaching, they cannot avoid bad assessment (Boud 1995). Boud and Falchikov (2007) point out that assessment is also a major concern and burden for those teaching students and suggest HEIs are afraid to change assessment systems because of the risks and major effort entailed, leading to slow incremental change, compromise, and inertia. The aspiration for innovative assessment approaches to provide ways of redefining assessment "as an instrument of liberation" (Bryan & Clegg 2006, p.1) for both students and HEIs may prove elusive within the realities, challenges, and constraints of organisations.

While the value of different forms of technology-based or e-assessment and their potential for offering learning benefits to students, through more frequent and immediate feedback, has been recognised, the design and implementation of e-assessments brings major challenges for HEIs (Whitelock 2009). Computer assisted assessment (CAA), encompassing computer-based assessment (CBA) and web-based assessment (WBA), offers immediate scoring and feedback to students and the potential to reduce the marking workload of educators. Initial start-up costs are associated with question authoring and review, and development of question banks (Ricketts & Wilks 2002; Deutsch et al 2012). Securing and maintaining support of University services including computing, estates, administration and quality assurance (Bull 1999) also needs to be factored in to development and running costs. But once the technologies and systems are in place, benefits can be realised for students, with online scoring enabling faster and more regular feedback, and for organisations, with automated marking and feedback offering human resource efficiencies, reducing marking workloads and ensuring greater accuracy at the point of marking.

CAA is associated with provision of multiple choice questions (MCQs) (Bull & Danson 2004). Once a databank of questions has been developed, the technology enables items to be selected for online delivery, automated scoring and feedback, and report generation. This type of assessment has been described as 'objective' but Biggs and Tang (2007, p.203) argue that it is 'not more scientific' or any less prone to error. The potential for error has simply moved from the point of marking to the point of authoring questions and response options; this is not necessarily any less subjective than assessing an essay or student presentation. Further the value of MCQs to test anything beyond basic knowledge has been challenged. Biggs and Tang (2007) suggest that while well-designed MCQs can assess higher order learning they are rarely developed in this way. Breadth of learning required to answer lots of questions challenges the value of MCQs for depth of understanding and as a means of assessment *for* learning. Biggs (2007, p. 238) articulates the dangers of CAA where it is used to reinforce the idea that 'knowing more' is equated with good learning. The pedagogical foundations for a constructively aligned curriculum where assessment strategies, learning activities and learning outcomes are clearly aligned are at risk if CAA adopters cannot rise to the challenge of designing and delivering more sophisticated questions that can assess higher order learning. The yin/yang of CAA is highlighted here with its main advantages apparently lying in more efficient assessment procedures bringing organisational and logistical benefits for assessing large student numbers through technology but calling into question its pedagogical value and effectiveness.

Audience response systems (ARS) have been employed in a range of subjects and described as a viable and flexible tool for engaging students in more active learning in classroom settings (Medina et al 2008), by providing rapid feedback about understandings, misunderstandings and clarification (Miller & Hartung 2012, Cain & Robinson 2008), and for testing and evaluation (Mareno et al 2010). Caldwell (2007, p. 2) advises that usage in 'summative high-stakes testing' is rare. ARS, or electronic voting systems (EVS) enable participants to respond to MCQs displayed to the whole class (Draper 2009). The aggregated answers, which can be presented using a variety of formats, for example, bar charts or pie charts, are displayed on screen for all to see how responses are distributed across options. But as with CAA, the pedagogical value of ARS is also questionable, relying as it does on using MCQs. Draper (2009, p.286-287) describes how the MCQ format has been associated with game shows like "Who wants to be a millionaire?" where questions are based on 'the lowest kind of learning' of disconnected facts but goes on to identify learning designs that can transcend this apparent disadvantage.

Various claims have been made about online methods of developing skills of critical reflection and critical thinking through discussion boards and blogs. In dental education Wetmore et al (2010) found that whilst blogs did not appear to enhance grades they improved levels of reflection and Hanson (2011) indicated that blogging encouraged group engagement. Goldman et al (2008) evaluated public health students' use of assessed weekly seminar blogs, highlighting opportunities for increased interaction, participation and learning. Students positively evaluated "exchanges with other students, hearing different perspectives, flexibility of time of participation, having other students see and comment on their postings and opinions, helping them stay on top of class work" (Goldman et al 2008, p.2). The ability for technology to provide interactivity and asynchronicity complements the opportunity it also brings for peer-to-peer collaborative learning. Fischer et al (2011) compared traditional written assignments to a group blog in medical education, with levels of reflection being comparable in both groups, going some way to demonstrate that deeper learning can be facilitated and evidenced through online shared spaces as well as the more traditional private assignment writing.

The objective of this study is to examine the design, implementation and impacts of innovative assessment strategies, with CAA, ARS and blogging, using analyses of student assessments and student and staff evaluations to identify the effects on student learning and the implications for educators. This will lead to a discussion of the yin and yang of innovative assessment, highlighting contrasts and connections between the controlled, systematic measurement and objectivity associated with multiple choice assessments, compared with the formative, iterative and subjective nature of reflective blogging and differences between individual and group assessment.

2. Context and method: Collaborative lifeworld-led learning strategies

The introduction of innovative assessment strategies form an integral part of a collaborative lifeworld-led transprofessional curriculum delivered to cohorts of 600 students in health and social work where technology has been harnessed to provide a multi-layered blended learning experience, connecting learners to humanising perspectives for guiding their practice. Assessment technologies included use of group blogs facilitated through Blackboard^{TM}, CAA using Questionmark Perception^{TM} and ARS using TurningPoint^{TM}. The innovative assessment strategies are situated within an undergraduate Year 2 unit, *Exploring Evidence to Guide Practice* (EE2GP). The humanising philosophy underpinning the unit encouraged students to integrate understandings about different kinds of knowledge for practice; conventional evidence, understandings about the person's experience, and the student's personal insights that come from imagining 'what it is like' for the person experiencing human services (Galvin & Todres 2011). This was facilitated through a series of 17 web-based case studies providing topic-related resources for learners to consider experiences of specific illnesses and conditions, such as dementia, social isolation, and substance misuse through narratives and poems, topic-specific qualitative and quantitative research, and policy and practice issues (Pulman et al 2012). These resources were supplemented with face-to-face (f2f) lectures and group work.

The intended learning outcomes were constructively aligned with the case study resources and teaching and learning strategies (Biggs & Tang 2007). The students were directed through weekly student managed guided learning (SMGL) activities over a four week period (Figure 1) using a detailed guide with tasks and questions to structure and scaffold their learning involving reading, listening, and viewing in preparation for critical reflection and blogging.

Case Studies in eLearning

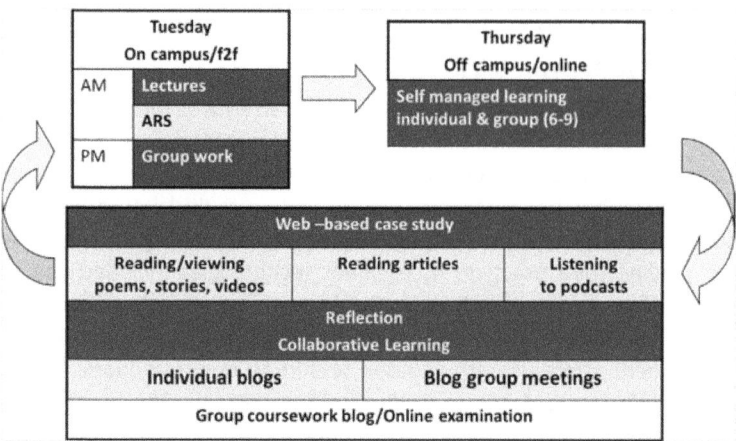

Figure 1: Weekly student experience

Firstly students were asked to explore what a health or social care condition or situation might be like for people experiencing it by reading and viewing stories, poems, and videos as evidence drawn from the arts and humanities. Secondly, students were asked to examine published research embedded within practice issues relevant to their field through reading and comparing a number of case study, topic-specific, research papers and listening to research active staff, talk about research through short podcasts. Thirdly, students were asked to consider how these different kinds of evidence could usefully guide their practice by comparing, reflecting and demonstrating their knowledge, facilitated by group work, which took place face-to-face and through the group blogs.

Students, working in groups of six to nine, were allocated case studies relevant to their field of study, Opportunities for considering transprofessional issues of what is required in humanly sensitive care, and associated tensions, risks and dilemmas were facilitated through inter-group discussions. Students, working in their groups, compiled and submitted individual blogs as formative coursework based on the weekly SMGL activities and received online formative feedback from educators. The purpose of the weekly activities was to enable students to build their knowledge progressively and collaboratively towards the summatively assessed group coursework blog (50%) and online MCQ examination (50%) at the end of the unit.

Building on projects supported by the Higher Education Academy (HEA) (Hutchings et al. 2011) and JISC/SEDA (Hutchings et al 2010b), this study examines the contributions of different forms of assessment to student learning through analysis of student assessment, feedback and evaluation. Data was collected over a two year period (2011 and 2012) using ARS voting pads to collect regular in-class feedback on the experience of undertaking the unit and an online end of unit evaluation, tailored to the specific features of the unit. The unit was delivered in two blocks each year with approximately 300 students per block. Data will be identified by cohort year 2011 and 2012 and block numbers 1 and 2, ie. 2011.1. The end of unit evaluation included, firstly, a set of item statements using a 5-point Likert scale from Strongly Agree to Strongly Disagree; secondly, a series of open response questions asking what "enhanced learning", what "challenged learning", what they "enjoyed most", what they "enjoyed least" and "recommendations for change". This was deployed immediately following the online examination and engendered very high response rates; 2011.1 98% (n=301), 2011.2 94% (n=243), 2012.1 86% (n=188) and 2012.2 94% (n=283). Staff evaluation was conducted by means of a staff focus group in 2011 and a questionnaire in 2012. Ethical processes and procedures were followed.

3. Findings: Adoption of innovative assessment strategies

The design, implementation and impacts of the innovative assessment strategies adopted will be examined in preparation for discussion of the challenges and implications for student learning, pedagogy, and organisation. The technologies deployed included CAA, ARS, and group blogs, affording combinations of assessment *for* learning and assessment *of* learning. We will examine the contributions of each of these in turn and relate these to our findings.

3.1. Computer assisted assessment (CAA)

The online MCQ examination consisted of 30 questions, 25 generic research questions and 5 case study specific questions, randomised by question and by options. Questions were presented one at a time and students were able to navigate between questions by using buttons to review their responses before submission. Students were given one hour to complete the exam; there was an on-screen timer and the exams were invigilated. Students were provided with copies of the journal articles they had read for their case studies.

The technology interface can impact on student acceptance and student performance in CAA. Ricketts and Wilks (2002) found the student assessment interface has a major impact on how acceptable CAA is to students with question-by-question delivery improving student performance compared with paper tests marked with OMR, where they identified a small improvement, and online scrolling, where they identified a large difference. Did the nature of the CAA assessment strategy impact on the student experience in this study? Student experiences of the online MCQ examination are identified in Table 1, which lists assessment-related item responses collated from the End of unit evaluation Likert-scale statements. The majority of students were positive about logging on to the MCQ examination (item1) and the user interface with questions identified as easy to read and answer on screen (item 2).

Table 1: End of unit evaluation statements

Item	End of unit evaluation statements		2011.1	2011.2	2012.1	2012.2
1.	Logging on to the multiple choice exam was easy and straightforward	Disagree/strongly disagree	61%	4%	19%	14%
		Agree/strongly agree	11%	86%	61%	63%
2.	The questions were easy to read and answer on the computer screen	Disagree/strongly disagree	48%	12%	11%	16%
		Agree/strongly agree	10%	70%	66%	60%

3.	Using computerised tests would be appropriate for other summative assessment in my course	Disagree/strongly disagree	27%	9%	13%	17%
		Agree/strongly agree	35%	58%	58%	49%
4.	I would prefer the assessment for this unit to be a 3,000 word essay on applying research evidence to practice	Disagree/Strongly disagree	81%*	71%*	69%	66%
		Agree/strongly agree	19%*	18%*	9%	13%
5.	I preferred submitting the group coursework assessment on the computer rather than on paper	Disagree/strongly disagree	16%	9%	13%	10%
		Agree/strongly agree	56%	62%	59%	57%
6.	The group blog has been helpful for learning collaboratively with my group	Disagree/strongly disagree	**	**	27%	30%
		Agree/strongly agree	**	**	48%	35%

* Statement 4 was included in the ARS for 2011.1 but not the end of unit evaluation.
** Statement 6 was not included in the end of unit evaluation for 2011.

But our findings also reveal that technical issues impacted adversely on student perceptions of CAA. A comparison of results for 2011.1 (items 1-3) compared with the other cohorts highlights the effects of technical issues experienced with logging on to the exam using a lockdown browser which delayed exam start times and added to exam anxiety for the 2011.1 block. Deutsch et al (2012) found that a positive CAA experience effects positive attitudinal changes towards the role of CBA, perceived ease of use and perceived objectivity. Our findings agree in showing that those students (2011.1) who experienced difficulties with the technology when accessing the online examination were less likely to agree that using computerised tests would be appropriate for other summative assessment (item 3).

Building student familiarity with innovative types of assessment is an important factor with students concerned:

Having to revise for a test, which is something I am not used to as I am used to preparing presentations, essays etc.(2012.1)

Students were given opportunities weekly to practice MCQ questions and receive feedback in lectures using the ARS. This enabled learning through shared feedback contributing to assessment *for* learning. Additionally a formative online mock assessment, consisting of 20 questions, was provided for students to familiarise themselves with the CAA interface in preparation for the summative online examination. But the challenges of the online MCQ examination were relative with the majority of students in all four cohorts identifying a preference for the innovative assessment strategies adopted in this unit over the more traditional and familiar 3,000 word essay (item 4).

3.2. Audience response system (ARS)

The ARS was used in the lecture theatre, with groups of approximately 300 students with the dual purpose of gathering opinion and gauging knowledge; through ongoing responses on the experience of the unit and formative self-assessment in exam preparation. Whilst it enabled students to experience typical MC exam questions and to gain rapid feedback and clarification it did not provide the facility for multiple responses as would be included in the exam. The overall trend, identified in Caldwell's (2007) literature review, is that, on the whole, students and educators like the ARS, but effectiveness is dependent on the pedagogic strategies informing their use (Cain & Robinson 2008; Draper 2009). In our evaluation student responses ranged from those who valued the learning opportunities provided to those who preferred less use of the ARS. The 2012.2 cohort were the most positive in their responses, recommending more usage of the ARS. The ability of the ARS to provide interactivity in large groups, to be enjoyable and provide feedback in order to check learning in preparation for the exam themes were noted by students, with the ARS providing a bridge between the process of learning, and the outcomes of that learning. The number of questions each week using the ARS was reduced in the 2012 cohort, taking into account response times needed to register the votes for such a large group.

The voting pads in lectures made my learning more interactive and engaged my attention so I thought this was useful. (2011.1)

The voting pads were fun, and really made me think about what I did and didn't know. (2012.1)

3.3. Group blogs

The group blog facility was part of the standard provision in the University's VLE, enabling the large cohort to be allocated to subgroups of 6-9, with a requirement for weekly individual formative blog contributions with the facility for intergroup comment and discussion, culminating in a final summative group blog. It was complemented by weekly face-to-face group work, with an opportunity to share learning with another group. The feedback from students on the helpfulness of the blogs for learning collaboratively indicated that whilst positive comments outweighed negative comments (Table 1, item 6) there was no strong trend in either direction. Themes in the responses included the opportunity to gather other opinions and learn from and with peers, acknowledging the opportunity for collaborative learning, whist some expressed preferences for an individualised approach with expectations of individual feedback and a preference for an individual rather than group mark.

Learning more about how others interpret the same material and in some ways it improved my understanding if there was something I was unsure of. (2012.2)

> The group blog and posting individual blogs every week helped me to reflect on what I had learnt. The smgl were useful in informing what you had to complete each week. (2011.1)

Some spoke of tensions within the subgroups in managing both the process and the product of the blog, with others recognising that learning to work effectively in groups represents the reality of health or social care practice. Some appeared to embrace the use of blogs whist others commented on the unfamiliarity with blogs as an educational tool.

Staff feedback indicated that the group blog was:

> ...better for assessing 'integration' and 'reflective ability', academic and professional skills that are important for the course's central topic: 'exploring evidence for practice'.

4. Discussion and conclusions

Student statements in the end of unit evaluations reveal significant ying/yang connections and interrelationships at work in the student experiences of innovative technology-enhanced assessment. The dynamic between breadth and depth of knowledge required and relationships between teaching and learning were clearly demonstrated. Students were challenged both by the depth of knowledge suggesting it was "complicated to understand" (2011.1) and "extremely difficult" (2012.1) and by its breadth:

> The exam has challenged me; it was a lot of information to take in in 5 weeks as it is such a broad subject (2011.1)

> There was so much information I needed to know, I felt very overwhelmed! (2011.1)

Gibbs (2006, p.18) argues where CAA is included as a component of assessment, "students tend to adopt a surface approach to their studies (attempting to reproduce) rather than a deep approach (trying to make sense)", pointing to potential adverse impacts of CAA assessment strategies on student learning. However it is significant that student comments relating to this assessment strategy were associated as much with it being an exam as being facilitated through technology, reflected in a student response to "what I enjoyed least":

The exam, just because it was an exam! (2011.2)

Notwithstanding exam anxiety as a factor, the MCQ assessment, consisting as it does of many questions on multiple topics, challenges the relationship between breadth and depth and highlights the importance of designing questions for deep learning and balancing breadth (numbers of questions) with depth (levels of difficulty). The yin yang features and benefits of CAA were identified by a member of staff:

It was efficient in that it tested both breadth and depth, covering a range of learning that was wider than I believe an essay would do. I also believe that it was efficient because it reduces the assessment burden on students (compared to a longer assignment), thus freeing their time for learning.

Further, the assessed discursive group blogs provided a dynamic counterbalance and complementarity to the controlled, time-limited and 'objective' exam. Informed by the unit philosophy of active, collaborative and reflective learning, in line with the shift from teaching to learning, it helps to address the concern that MCQ examinations do not facilitate deep learning. The ARS acted as a focal point for monitoring research knowledge and understanding and facilitating interactivity, with potential to be used more to facilitate collaborative and constructivist learning through students working together to debate and choose answers.

Our findings also highlight the dynamics of relationships between teaching and learning and the impact of technology, where students recommended reverting to familiar face-to-face lecture and seminar strategies to improve their exam preparedness:

I would have preferred to have structured seminars to prepare us better for the examination. (2012.2)

Some students appeared to have unrealistic expectations of the technology or concerns about its reliability and some emphasised technical problems, potential and real, rather than the capacity to learn or be assessed differently. Technology was afforded considerable potential yet subjected to scrutiny and criticism with user acceptance fluctuating according to perceived and actual experiences. Readiness for technology-enhanced assessment strategies appeared to be linked to the predominant learning culture with a lag between what was technically feasible but risky and what was accepted. Benefits can be longer term, as Wyllie (2011) discovered that students who engaged in online learning and assessment became more independent learners, taking more responsibility for their own and their peers' learning.

The multi-layered blended learning strategy underpinning the unit sought to balance efficiencies with effectiveness, face-to-face on-campus and online off-campus teaching and learning, group and individual learning, discursive and MCQ assessment, employing a range of technology enhanced modes of assessment. Student feedback drew attention to passive and active approaches to learning, particularly in relation to group participation, face-to-face and online. In developing such a complex approach it is important for HEIs "not to be dazzled or seduced by what the technology can do but to adapt and apply" it to what we want students to be able to do (Quinney 2005, p. 449) in a more radical shift from just replacing current teaching and learning strategies to transforming the process of learning, in line with the constructivist pedagogy and learning theory at the root of the EE2GP unit. Hutchings et al (2010a, p.201), in an earlier study, drew attention to experiences of educators who may be uncertain or unconvinced of the efficacy of disruptive technologies in teaching and learning concluding that "the challenge is to achieve 'optimum disruption', where transformation is seen as achievable and realistic, rather than being experienced as too uncomfortable". These challenges and associated risks must be addressed through strategic engagement and co-partnering, at institution, school, programme and unit levels, with management, staff and students, in order to change cultures and practices.

5. Acknowledgements

Development and evaluation of the EE2GP unit was supported by the HEA Discipline-focused Learning Technology Enhancement Academy (Hutchings et al 2011) and project funding from JISC/SEDA Embedding Work-with-IT (Hutchings et al. 2010b).

References

Biggs, J. and Tang, C. (2007) Teaching for Quality Learning at University, 3rd ed. Society for Research into Higher Education & Open University Press.

Boud, D. (1995) Enhancing Learning through Self Assessment, London: Kogan Page.

Boud, D. and Falchikov. N. (2007) Rethinking Assessment in Higher Education, London: Routledge.

Bryan, C. and Clegg, K. (2006) Innovative Assessment in Higher Education, London, Routledge.

Bull, J. (1999). "Computer-assisted Assessment: Impact on Higher Education institutions", Educational Technology & Society, Vol. 2, No. 3, pp 123-126.

Bull, J. and Danson, M. (2004) Computer-assisted Assessment (CAA), LTSN Generic Centre Assessment Series No 14.

Cain, J. and Robinson, E. (2008) "A Primer on Audience Response Systems; Current Applications and Future Considerations, American Journal of Pharmaceutical Education, Vol 72, No.4, p 77.

Caldwell, J.E. (2007). "Clickers in the Large Classroom: Current Research and Best Practice", Life Sciences Education, Vol. 6, No.1, pp 9-20.

Deutsch, T., Herrmann, K. Frese, T. and Sandholzer, H. (2012) Implementing Computer-based Assessment: a Web-based Mock Examination Changes Attitudes. Computers & Education, Vol. 58, No. 4, pp 1068-1075.

Draper, S.W. (2009) "Catalytic Assessment: Understanding how MCQs and EVS can Foster Deep Learning", British Journal of Educational Technology, Vol. 40, No. 2, pp 285-293.

Fischer, M.A., Haley, H.L., Saarinen, C.L. and Chretien, K.C. (2011) "Comparison of Blogged and Written Reflections in two Medicine Clerkships", Medical Education, Vol. 45, No.2, pp 166-75.

Galvin, K and Todres, L. (2011) "Research Based Empathic Knowledge for nursing: a Translational Strategy for Disseminating Phenomenological Research Findings to Provide Evidence for Caring", International Journal of Nursing Studies, Vol. 48, No. 4, pp 522-530.

Gibbs, G. (2006) "How Assessment Frames Student Learning", In Bryan, C. and Clegg, K. Innovative Assessment in Higher Education, London, Routledge. pp 23-36.

Goldman, R.H. Cohen, AP, Sheahan, F. 2008."Using Seminar Blogs to Enhance Student Participation and Learning in Public Health School Classes", American Journal of Public Health, Vol, 98,No. 9, pp 1658-1663.

Hanson, K. (2011). "Blog Enabled Peer-to-peer Learning", Journal of Dental Education, Vol. 85, No. 91, pp 6-12.

Hutchings, M., Quinney, A. & Scammell, J. (2010a) "The Utility of Disruptive Technologies in Interprofessional Education: Negotiating the Substance and Spaces of Blended Learning", In Bromage, A. et al. (Eds) Interprofessional eLearning and Collaborative Work: Practices and Technologies. Hershey, PA: IGI.

Hutchings, M., Galvin, K., Todres, L., Quinney, A., Pulman, A., Atkins, P. & Gentle, P. (2010b). "Transformational Change through Lifeworld-led Multimedia VLE engagement", Embedding Work-with-IT Final Report. Bournemouth University and the Leadership Foundation for Higher Education for JISC/SEDA.

Hutchings, M., Galvin, K., Pulman, A., Todres, L., Quinney, A., Clark, V. and Atkins, P. (2011). Framing Lifeworld-led Evidence to Shape Practice: Facilitating a Collaborative Transprofessional Curriculum for Health and Social Work Disciplines. Final Report for Higher Education Academy Discipline-focused Learning Technology Enhancement Academy. Bournemouth University.

Mareno, N., Bremner, M. and Emerson, C. (2010) "The Use of Audience Response Systems in Nursing Education: Best Practice Guidelines", International Journal of Nurse Education Scholarship, Vol. 7, No.1,

Medina, M.S., Medina, P.J., Wanzer, D.S Wilson, J.E. and Briton, M,L. (2008) "Use of an Audience Response System (ARS) in a Dual-campus Classroom Environment", American Journal of Pharmaceutical Education, Vol. 72, No.2, p 38.

Miller, M. and Hartung, S.Q. (2012) "Evidence-based Clicker Use: Audience Response Systems for Rehabilitation Nurses", Rehabilitation Nursing, Vol.37, No.3, pp 151-159.

Polkinghorne, D. (2004) Practice and the human sciences: The case for a judgment-based practice of care, Albany, N.Y. State University of New York Press.

Pulman, A.J., Galvin, K., Hutchings, M., Todres, L., Quinney, A., Ellis-Hill, C. and Atkins, P. (2012) "Empathy and Dignity through Technology: using Lifeworld-led Multimedia to Enhance Learning about the Head, Heart and Hand". Electronic Journal of e-Learning. Forthcoming.

Quinney, A. (2005). "Placements Online: Student Experiences of a Website to Support Learning in Practice Settings", Social Work Education, Vol. 24, No.4, pp439-450.

Ricketts, C. (2002) "Improving Student Performance through Computer-based Assessment: Insights from Recent Research", Assessment & Evaluation in Higher Education, Vol. 27, No. 5, pp 475-479.

Wetmore, A.O., Boyd, L.D., Bowen, D.M. and Patillo, R.E. (2010). "Reflective Blogs in Clinical Education to Promote Critical Thinking in Dental Hygiene Students", Journal of Dental Education. Vol. 74, No. 12, pp1337-1350.

Whitelock, D. (2009) Editorial: E-assessment: Developing New Dialogues for the Digital Age. British Journal of Educational Technology, Vol. 40, No. 2, pp 199-202.

Wyllie. A .(2011) "Eager 'weavers': Designing Assessment for an Online Environment", Nurse Education Practitioner, Vol. 11, No. 2, pp 99-103.

E-Enablement in Distance Education – Engineering Growth: A Case Study of IMT-CDL

Tushar Marwaha and Anita Mathew
IMT-Centre for Distance Learning, Ghaziabad, UP, India

Editorial Commentary
E-learning first began to show its potential in the field of distance education, where learners and teachers were, by necessity, physically separate. This paper looks at such a context in India, where there is a growing demand for part-time distance education in management for employed professionals unable to attend classes on campus. The role of Information technology in this context must be professional and efficient, to fit with the demands of learners. This case study investigates the extent to which technology readiness, as measured by an Index judging optimism, innovativeness, discomfort and insecurity concerning technology use in all circumstances, may affect the way professionals adapt to an e-enabled learning environment in India. Questionnaires on ICT skills and social media tools were emailed to students, with the majority of respondents being IT professionals, used to using these tools. Questions remain as to whether social media tools familiar for work and personal life will deliver for learning.

Abstract: In today's environment, educated professionals are the need of the hour. Since it's not practical for everyone to go through full-time management courses, distance education is a good option. But, bringing together educators and students from across the world, with all manners of learning, experience, requirements and skill set deficiencies isn't easy. For this, e-enablement is being increasingly looked upon as a saviour. Use of e-resources allows institutions to touch base with an ever increasing number of students in an efficient and effective manner. E-resources like videoconferencing, interactive learning, social media tools and distributable notes are being adopted by distance and full-time campuses alike. This allows distance educators to be available more of the time and to more of the students. Factors like a steady increase in the adoption of the internet, portable computing, a deepening comfort level with technology and the entry of professional education firms in this domain are helping to cement e-resources as a viable teaching tool in the minds of the educators and students alike. However, simply having the infrastructure in place is not good enough if adoption and comfort levels are not up to the mark. Institute of Management Technology – Centre for Distance Learning (IMT-CDL) is a pioneer in the field of management education via distance learning. It has managed to steadily increase both the number of tools on offer and their respective utilization levels, thereby delivering a better learning experience. This study attempts to focus on the adoptability of e-enablement in distance education. For a practical perspective, we would be using our experience as coordinators for the online courses offered by IMT-CDL when examining the factors and their impact for the same. It will also be used for examining the past and for exploring avenues for the future of e-resources in distance education.

Keywords: eLearning, ICT, distance learning, IMT-CDL, social media

1. Executive summary

Purpose/Objectives – The study aims to assess the respondents' e-skills levels and psychology towards the use of technology for academic purposes and suitable tools thereof. This will help in determining the feasibility of using e-enabled resources (ICT's) for enhancing the quality of the educational offerings in the Indian distance learning scenario.

Design/Methodology/Approach – Two questionnaires were developed to collect data, one for assessing the feasibility of using social media tools for enhancing student-institution interaction and one for analysing the ICT skills level of the respondents. The questionnaire was circulated amongst 759 students who are enrolled in the PG level management courses offered by IMT-CDL through online mode, utilizing ICT tools for course delivery and management.

Findings – The survey found that a majority of respondents claimed to be tech-savvy and exhibited reasonably high levels of IL. Overall, 73.87% of the respondents claimed to be using ICT enabled services with a score of 3.81/5 on comfort levels and a confidence level of

75.52%. Among social media tools, Facebook and Google Groups clock in at 3.93 and 3.63 (scale of 5) respectively as feasible tools for interaction and e-enablement of learning. Overall, there is a favourable response to e-enablement.

Practical Implications – The study provides glimpses into the psychology of learners (primarily working professionals) enrolled in PG level management courses via distance learning. This will in turn help in structuring course and learning methodology offerings to maximize learning and improve the learning experience for the students. Use of ICT tools is imperative.

2. Introduction

"Men learn from one another. But all learning is only the exchange of material. No man can give another the capacity to think. Yet that capacity is our only means of survival." (Rand 1952)

Education is all about the shaping of the mind, a process of "culturalization" that forms the bedrock for civilization as we know of it today. The pursuit of education and knowledge have shaped human endeavour since the dawn of time; From the time the caveman discovered fire to today's cutting edge space research. But, efficacy matters. In distance education, the typical audience of a distance learning course is older, a working professional and usually pursuing a course for career advancement. For people like this, is it education or learning that is more relevant? And how do we bring that learning closer to them, making it more effective and useful? This can be done by improving the existing learning system, motivating and connecting with the students on a more personal level. E-enablement can help.

3. Literature Review

Relevance of ELearning and ICT skills in a distance learning environment

Today, in India, the entire market for education is changing. With the coming of the BPO/KPO and ITeS boom in India, college graduates are easily getting jobs that pay anything between Rs. 12,000/- to Rs. 25,000/- p.m. as starting salary. There is no pressing need for them to go for higher education for about 4 to 5 years, until they hit the glass ceiling which excludes those who are not in possession of PG level qualifications in Management. This is when they start approaching distance learning institutions. A vast majority of the potential students are corporate professionals and they demand professionalism, time-bound delivery, flexibility, approachability, quality and long-term value.

Delivering this is not possible without the support of technology. ICT's (Information and Communication Technology enabled tools) are increasingly being considered or deployed worldwide to improve the education process and address problems related to declining education standards, rising costs, increasing students numbers and general increased demand for higher education. As Mutula (2002) identifies, universities are using ICT's like OPAC and WebCT to tap into the potential of campus intranets, libraries, online databases and other resources. Students can pursue independent project-based studies at a distance. Via eLearning it is possible for greater interaction to take place between student and instructor, allowing for a more intimate form of education. (Mutula 2002)

Distance teaching requires technologies that are cheap, reliable, easy to use, multifunctional and easily accessible to the majority of the learners. (Mutula 2002) Developing eLearning systems is an expensive exercise and its utilization and success hinges not only on the users' technology acceptance of an eLearning system, but also their state of technology readiness and prior ICT experience, among others. (Lai 2008) Since there is also a wide variety in terms of age, gender, reason(s) for joining such courses, educational background, work experience, learning potential, job role, physical location and devotion to studies, customizing eLearning resources is necessary. All these factors significantly impact the student-course sync-up of and affect his level of participation and take-homes. Also, having the best e-resources is redundant if the learners aren't comfortable or unable to make full use of the same.

With a view to understanding this we can use the technology readiness index (TRI) developed by Parasuraman and Rockbridge Associates, Inc. to measure technology readiness. Parasuraman (2000) defined technology readiness as "people's propensity to embrace and use new technologies for accomplishing goals in home life and at work" (p. 308). People's beliefs about technology can be categorized into four distinct dimensions, namely, optimism, innovativeness, discomfort, and insecurity. (Mutula 2008, Westjohn et al 2009) Westjohn et al (2009) suggest that the first two be considered facilitators of technology usage, while the latter two are inhibitors of technology usage. Parasuraman (2000) suggests that those with a higher TRI rating were more likely to buy or sell stocks over the internet, use machines to purchase a plane or train ticket, own cell phones, and have internet access. Stretching this, any learner, who is able to perform these tasks, would be comfortable participating in an e-enabled learning environment. This is where IL (Information Literacy) becomes relevant. IL is "knowing when and why you need information, where to find it, and how to evaluate, use and communicate it in an ethical manner. (CILIP, 2010)". (Alireza and Vahideh 2011) The learning process, especially in the field of management, is now increasingly based on the capacity to find and access knowledge, and to apply it in problem solving. (Alireza and Vahideh 2011) There is a strong suggestion that IL would equip learners with the critical skills to become more independent lifelong learners, allowing them to master content and extend their investigations, become more self-directed and assume greater control over their own learning. (Salleh et al 2011) IL will also enable them to effectively utilize the e-enabled services being offered.

Westjohn et al (2009) suggest that the diffusion of global communication technology, e.g. websites, email, cellular phones, has enabled globally-oriented individuals to expand their sphere of living and gain exposure to the practices and standards of cultures far and wide. (Westjohn et al 2009) Thus both students and institutions can adopt global best practices and improve together. This can help distance learning providers expand their reach. The proliferation of technology-based products and services, and evidence of the challenges and frustrations associated with using them effectively, suggest an urgent need for scholarly inquiries on several important issues: How ready are people to embrace and effectively use new technologies? What are the primary determinants of technology readiness? Is it possible to group people into distinct segments on the basis of their technology readiness, and, if so, do those segments differ meaningfully on demographic, lifestyle, and other criteria? (Parasuraman 2000)

Ironically, although new technologies have been penetrating the population at increasing rates, evidence suggests signs of growing consumer frustration and disillusionment. (Parasuraman 2000) The promotion of digital literacy in particular, remains a major challenge facing most countries especially those in the developing world. It is important to deploy ICT-related skills through traditional education system because most business enterprises provide little or no formal training, and largely they tend to hire qualified staff. (Mutula 2002) But, this traditional system does not always give the desired results. Japan was an early promoter of the use of ICT in schools, and in 1994 began with the 100 schools project (United Nations Educational, Scientific & Cultural Organization (UNESCO) 2008). Despite its first-rate infrastructure, Japan has actually fallen from 17th to 19th place in the World Bank's Knowledge Economy Index (KEI) rankings, a measure of the success of ICT implementation (World Bank 2008), thus suggesting that outlay for equipment and subsequent ease of access does not necessarily result in increased use (Ono & Zavodny 2007). (Elwood and Maclean 2009)

The key problem here is the cross-connection of sorts that exists between the learners and instructors/teachers. Today's students – K through college (U.S. pattern) – have spent their entire lives surrounded by and using computers, videogames, digital music players, video cams, cell phones, and all the other toys and tools of the digital age. Today's average college grads have spent less than 5,000 hours of their lives reading, but over 10,000 hours playing video games (not to mention 20,000 hours watching TV). They are the Digital Natives while the instructors are Digital Immigrants. These instructors, who speak an outdated language (that of the pre-digital age), are struggling to teach a population that speaks an entirely new language. (Prensky 2001) Unfortunately, as Elwood and Maclean (2009) point out, training for existing teachers lags behind this outlay of resources. In 2006, Japan's National Institute of Multimedia Education (NIME) surveyed 880 tertiary education institutions and found that only some 30% had implemented faculty development for using ICT (NIME 2007).

Utilizing ICT tools has its own pitfalls. Skolnik and Puzo's (2008) research suggests that while both students and faculty feel that laptops were more effective; the faculty felt overwhelmed and the students had attention issues. Assignment evaluation encountered increased instances of academic dishonesty and if students are taught using ICT tools and then sit for pen-and-paper exams, the effectiveness of both the learning and evaluation process are at stake. Using ICT tools is good for enhancing learning experience but proper execution is required.

Above all, as Hamid (2001) points out, although computer usage and internet access are growing spectacularly in many parts of the world, "it remains the case that little more than 5 per cent of the world's population are internet users and, 88 per cent of these are in the industrialised countries."

It is estimated that approximately 75 per cent of all Internet information is produced in just one language, English. This may hurt e-enablement in non-native English speaking countries (a vast majority are located in the developing third-world where many educational systems are struggling with imparting basic learning, but for whom eLearning platforms would be very beneficial – it's a vicious circle of sorts). Cooperation as well as collaboration among all related bodies in the education system are key to lessening the obstacles to IL (Alireza and Vahideh 2011) and consequently the growth of eLearning as a viable tool for the education sector.

It is important that we realise that eLearning will be complementary to, but not fundamentally alter, the elements of teaching. eLearning should be perceived as a re-engineering process. (Mutula 2002) The way forward could be with blended learning. This mixes student learning through traditional face-to-face teaching integrating with an online learning management system (LMS). (Sen 2011) These practices are becoming the basis for much of today's academics. But, there is complexity in terms of the wide variety of settings and the diversity of the student population. (Sen 2011) We must look at the needs of the learners while designing an e-enabled system.

3.1. Distance Learning Environment in India

Table 1: Needs of the learners

Individual Perspective	Corporate Perspective
Need of qualifications for career growth.	Tool of motivation.
Unable to take a career break to pursue a full-time course.	Retention tool (when coupled with bonds/time-linked reimbursement plans).
Flexibility of learning.	Skill upgradation is encouraged.
Truncated commitment of time, money and effort.	Supplementing internal trainings.
For self-growth and skills enhancement.	Managing growth and innovation.
Only option (medical/locational reasons).	
Preparing for a career change (esp. Armed Forces officers).	

Table 2: Students' requirements from a distance education provider

Online classes via live videoconferencing.	Good faculty.
Availability of basic services via an e-enabled system.	Convenience to access the recorded lectures anytime.
Access to the slides and notes of the faculty.	More of automation
Above all, somebody should take the time and patience to deal with them properly and treat them and their queries with respect, providing proper information in a timely and professional manner.	Yet, they still want some sort of leeway to be given to them. (Harking to the concept of psychological excuses)

Distance education in India had historically suffered from "reputation paralysis" and was seen as the Cinderella of the Indian education sector. The coming of IGNOU (in 1985) and the changing economic scenario provided a fillip to this sector. Today, there are close to 197 institutions recognised by the statutory body, the DEC (Distance Education Council). (DEC 2012) There is a strategic shift towards e-enablement as the students are demanding a better learning experience. It must be understood that the distance education student is actually, psychologically, looking for excuses for both getting out of the course and for putting his head down and finishing the course. The onus is on educators for providing a motivating environment in which the student can gain knowledge and learn.

Table 1 and 2 depict the needs and requirements of the learners. The success of an e-enabled system is depends on the utilization of the facilities available, which are, in turn dictated by the needs of the students. Based on this, institutions can prepare their system accordingly.

ICT's and e-enabled systems can help by providing a platform for accessing basic services via website based systems, online classes via videoconferencing and improving student-institution interaction via social media tools. All of this effort would help in going global (in terms of locations) and tapping a wider audience base.

3.2. Evaluating the distance learning environment in India

A survey conducted by Careers 360 (2011) provides an insight into the distance learning environment in India. Table 3 helps depict this data.

The parameters for judging efficacy include course material, interaction levels, online support systems, conduct of the exams and results, response of the administration, teaching assistance, availability of faculty at the study centres, access to the study centres, and response time of the study centre. (Careers 360 2011)

Table 3: Rankings – Careers 360 Survey

Rank	Name of the Institution	Location	Resources & Reach (300)	Learning Experience (400)	Output (300)	Total (1000)
1	Indira Gandhi National Open University	New Delhi	205.31	258.12	198	661.43
2	Yashwantrao C. Maharashtra Open University	Nasik	145.2	239.54	233.16	617.9
3	IMT Distance and Open Learning Institute	Ghaziabad	40.55	285	258.14	583.69
4	Sikkim Manipal University	Gangtok	65.4	279.91	200.85	546.16
5	University of Mumbai	Mumbai	18.04	262.35	256.32	536.71
6	Maulana Azad National Urdu University	Hyderabad	59.71	215.91	249.17	524.79
7	Dr. B.R.Ambedkar Open University	Hyderabad	81.27	210	229.46	520.72
8	Symbiosis Centre for Distance Learning	Pune	31.98	240	235.5	507.48
9	Dr. Babasaheb Ambedkar Open University	Ahmedabad	31.66	220.8	246.23	498.68
10	Annamalai University	Annamalai Nagar	93.2	195	206	494.2

In a distance learning scenario, there is no or at best limited scope for interacting with the institution on a more personal level. The participants are globally dispersed, across divergent timezones and involved in all manner of job roles. This severely impacts their learning experience, reducing, in many cases, distance learning to simply an avenue that provides only a degree/qualification rather than learning and long-term, fruitful interactions. This connect between the students and institution is very important.

3.3. Using social media tools for enhancing student-institution interaction

Why do we need to interact with our students? To what extent should we interact with our students? Where do we draw the line between the student-faculty relationship? How effective are these interactions? Is this interaction/engagement really necessary? (Marwaha 2012) These questions are very relevant here. As traditional engagement models disappear, respect and attention need to be sought rather than demanded and the success of a faculty and the institution is increasingly being measured on the satisfaction levels of the students.

A feasible way of providing a good learning experience is through the use of social media tools like social networking (web)sites (SNS), using which the institution(s)/faculty could stay in touch with the students. It is a bi-directional process as students too are using these mediums to share comment to their teachers. (Musibau et al 2011) The question then arises is – which SNS tool(s) is/are the best suited for this purpose. There are many to choose from and they can be defined as "(Social networking sites are) online communities of Internet users who want to communicate with other users about areas of mutual interest, whether from a personal, business or academic perspective. The specific functionality of the various sites may differ, but in general, the sites allow users to provide information about them and communicate with others through email, chat rooms and other forums".(Pelgrin 2009)

Figure 1 helps depict the respondents' preferences. Since the focus is on ICT tools that provide two-way interaction, tools like YouTube, and integrators like Digg are being not covered. The tools under focus are Facebook, Twitter, Blooger.com, Google, Google Plus and Microsoft SkyDrive.

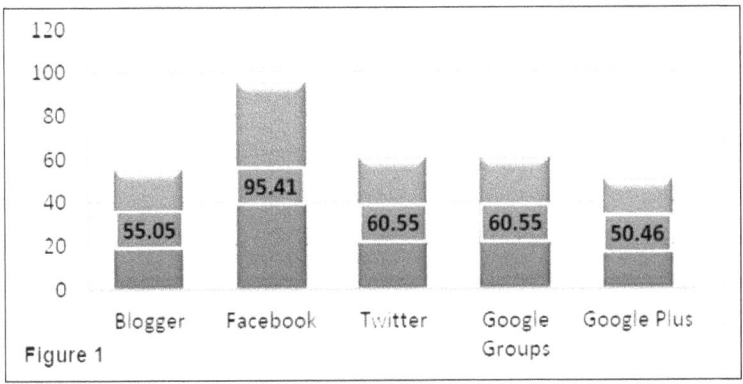

Figure 1: SNS usage at a personal level

Jain (2010) suggests that Facebook and Twitter are amongst the most popular SNS's. According to Alexa Site Stats-Global (2012) Facebook is the 2nd most popular website, behind Google.com and is the most popular SNS. Twitter comes in at rank 8 followed by Blogspot.com (a.k.a. Blogger.com) at 11. In India, Facebook is at 3rd with Twitter and Blogger.com coming in at rank 11 and 15 respectively. (Alexa 2012-India) A related survey in 2012 has Facebook at 2nd rank overall, behind leader Bebo.com. In terms of features, Facebook lags only behind MySpace.com. (TopTenReviews 2012)

3.4. Biopic of IMT-CDL

Established in 1986, IMT-CDL is a premier provider of distance education in the field of management in India. To supplement the growing student base, numerous technological innovations have been executed, creating improved interaction, bringing referrals, reducing dependency on the coordinator and inducing cost effectiveness. IMT-CDL offers many courses, out of which the Two Year Post Graduate

Diploma in Management (Online) and the One Year Post Graduate Diploma in Management (Executive) are taken for this study.

Tools like Google Groups, SkyDrive (Hotmail), Blog – www.imtcdlonlinecourses.blogspot.com, Facebook – https://www.facebook.com/imtcdlonlinecourses and Twitter – @IMTCDLOnline are used and these form a part of this survey.

4. Research methodology

Two questionnaires were designed and administered.

Questionnaire 1 (*I*) – ICT skills: This deals with ownership and usage patterns of ICT tools/services, comfort and confidence levels, abilities, psychological state, preferences, willingness to learn levels and demographic data. This was emailed to *759* students. A total of *150* complete and usable responses were logged at a response rate of *19.95 percent* (150/752). (Marwaha n.p. – b)

Questionnaire 2 (*II*) – Social media tools: This questionnaire deals with general usage patterns related to SNS's, the respondents' requirements, usage and awareness levels, tool-wise survey and demographic data. This was emailed to *572* students. A total of *109* complete and usable responses were logged at a response rate of *19.2 percent* (109/569). (Marwaha n.p. – a)

The questionnaires were inputted via the "Forms" feature in 'Google Docs' and sent/shared via email and Google Groups to the students enrolled in the two courses under study

5. Analysis

The data was analysed using the MS Excel (2007, SP3) package and simple statistical tools were considered. The data is presented with a simple visual perspective through graphs and tables as per requirements.

In Figure 2, the skew is towards "Young" and it's reflected in the responses. (Positive perception for e-enablement in education.)

Overall:
Total = 759
Gender Ratio = 0.293 (Females to Males)
Average Age = 29 (approx)
Youngest = 21
Eldest = 61
Data in Figure 3 supports this.

Respondents Profile

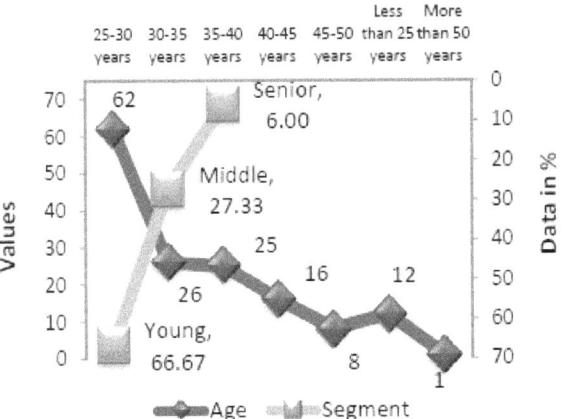

Figure 2: Age analysis
All are labelled with Questionnaire Number (e.g. II)

Case Studies in eLearning

Figure 3: Profession

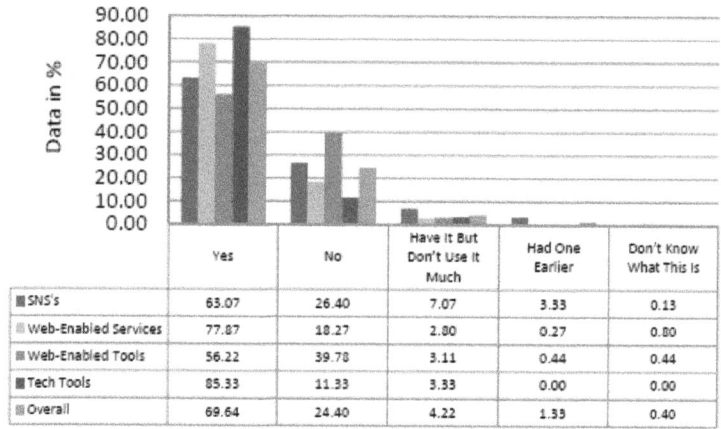

Figure 4: Tech services (usage)- group wise

The majority of the respondents are IT professionals and they would obviously be more comfortable using e-enabled systems. Based on this, analysing the tech competence of the respondents becomes easier.

(I) As Figure 4 suggests, a majority of the respondents are and have been using various e-enabled tools and services. The primary response here is "Yes".

(I) This gets reflected in their comfort levels as well. Figure 5 depicts this.

(I) Furthermore, we can judge the respondents' technical competence by looking at the ease with which they are able to perform tasks that utilise e-enabled systems. Figure 6 captures this data.

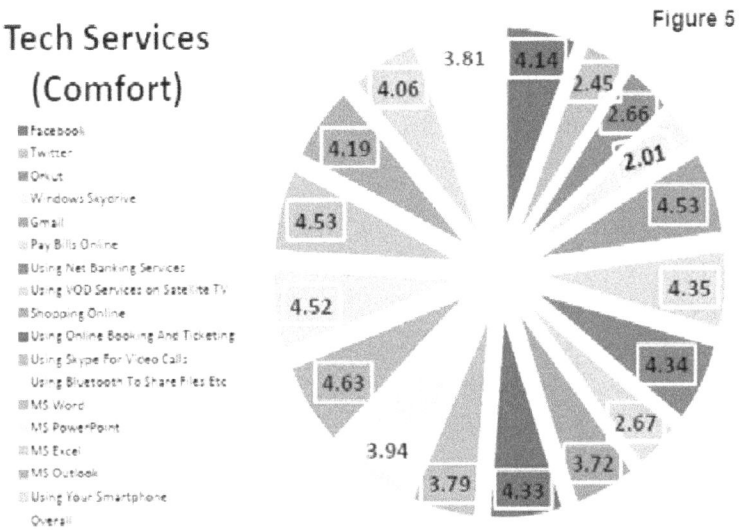

Figure 5: Tech services (comfort)

It is worth noting that using these services has induced many respondents to sign up and start using these SNS's. An overall picture is presented in Figure 7 and 8.

(II) Facebook tops, but Google Groups is considered to be the best tool overall (for interaction purposes), has the most scope for contribution and is the best utilized tool.

(II) We can now look at the usage patterns for the SNS's in extant use. This data is captured in Figure 8.

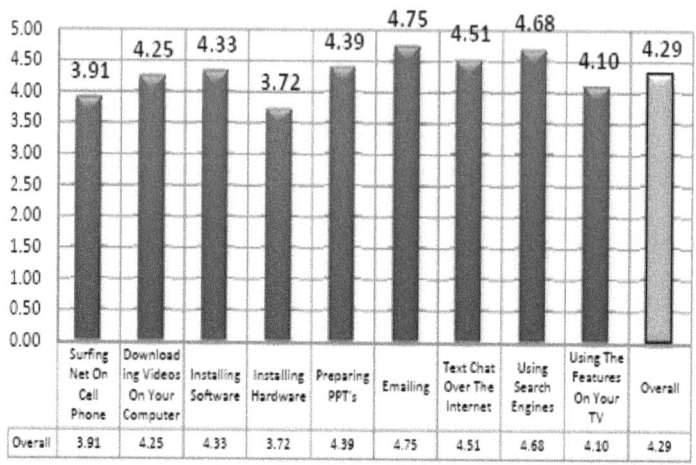

Figure 6: Tech competence

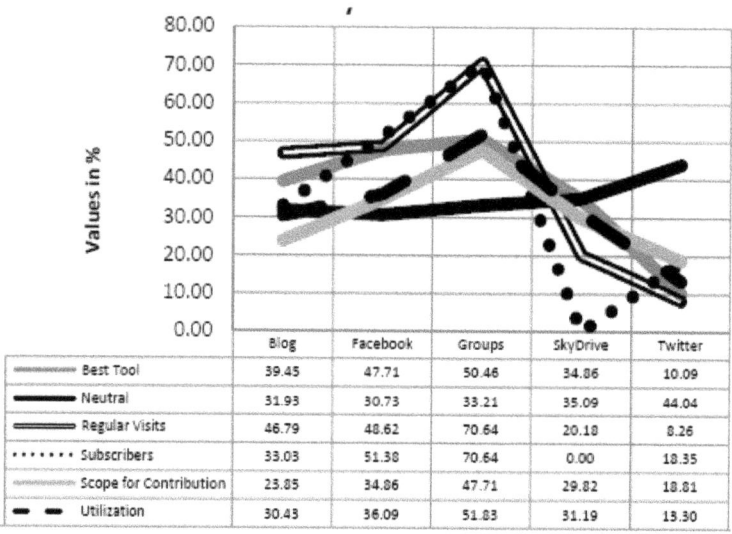

Figure 7: SNS study - overall

(I) Overall, we can safely say that the respondents' are tech savvy and are suitable/willing to use and work with e-enabled systems. This

would give a fillip to the development and subsequent roll-out of ICT enabled services for improving student-institution interactions.

Figure 9 presents a comprehensive picture.

(II) Overall, the respondents are quite happy with the SNS's in use as is reflected in Figure 10.

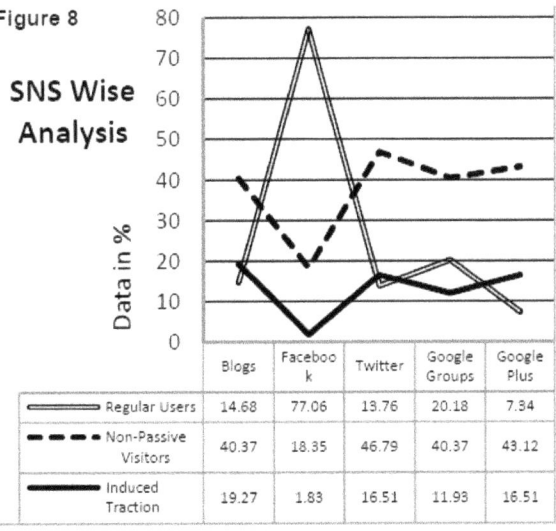

Figure 8: SNS wise analysis

Case Studies in eLearning

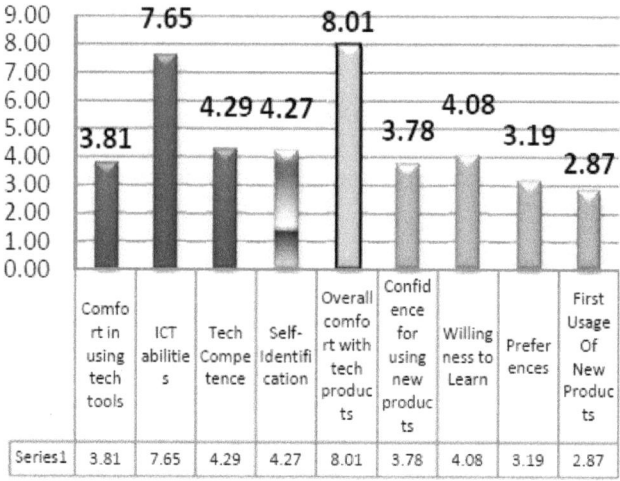

Figure 9: Overall analysis

6. Discussion

"I'm working to improve my methods, and every hour I save is an hour added to my life." (Rand 1952)

As mentioned earlier, the tools should sync-up with the needs of both, the students and the distance learning institution. As this data suggests, the respondents are quite happy with using the available tools. However, the large number (close to $1/3^{rd}$) "Neutral" responses in Figure 10 and the low score of 2.87 on 'First Usage of New Products' in Figure 8 are cause enough to pause and consider the amount of sync-up that is being generated. Individually, the respondents are tech savvy and comfortable, even appreciative of using ICT tools in education. Now what needs to be done is to link these up into a system that is both robust and useful for all involved. Of course, it is not possible to change everything all at once, prioritization needs to be done.

E-enablement and distance learning are partners in each other's growth and the changing education scenario is sure to provide suitable opportunities that encourage this partnership.

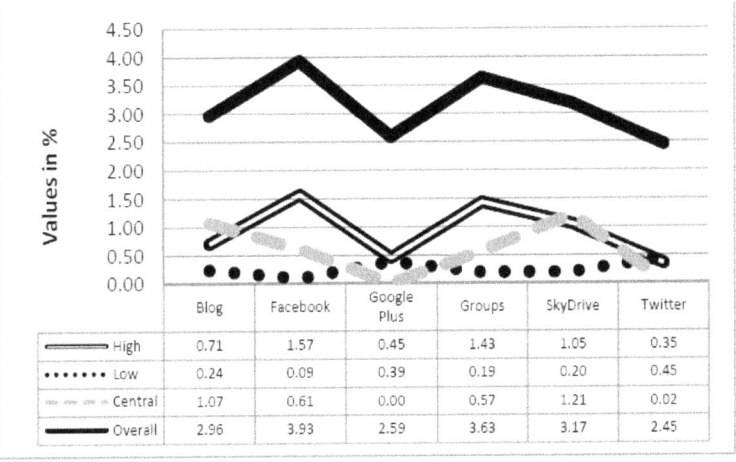

Figure 10: Overall effectiveness

The future of e-enablement for distance education

- Content publishers are customizing study material and providing eLearning tools.
- Multimedia content like videos and animations are increasing the levels of interaction.
- Tools like Moodle are combining many social tools into one easy to use and maintain system.
- More exposure to e-enabled tools has reduced the reluctance towards using them. As the data suggests, shifting to SNS enabled systems is forcing learners to start using SNS's.

7. Conclusion

The respondents to the study are quite tech savvy with a score of 8.01/10 on "Overall Comfort with Tech Products". They have also shown positive inclination towards the use of SNS's, giving them an overall score of *3.12/5*. As far as the feasibility goes, scores of *31.01/100* and *32.57/100* indicate that SNS's can be used for the intended purposes of improving the student-institution interaction, however, volumes are missing as the number of respondents is small and not everyone has the same level of e-skills. Lai's (2008) study also found similar results, stating that the usage of ICT, such as e-mail and the internet, was quite widespread among the respondents (professional accounting students in Malaysia). She also suggests that, pragmatically, professional students need to be taught how to use the internet, accounting software and eLearning system effectively in campus. (Lai 2008)

IMT-CDL has been able to implement e-enablement successfully, creating a positive image in the process. SNS's have been integrated with proprietary systems to add value to the learning process and the data supports this. However, there is still an immense distance to go, but a good start, a positive image in the minds of the students, syncing-up with the needs of the students and proper (i.e. utilizing the tools in a specific manner, focussing on the respective merits/intended usage of each) may prove stimulation enough for long-term growth and sustainability.

References

Alexa.com (1998) *Alexa Top 500 Global Sites*. [online] Available at: http://www.alexa.com/topsites/global [Accessed: 5 August 2012].

Alexa.com (1997) *Alexa - Top Sites in India*. [online] Available at: http://www.alexa.com/topsites/countries/IN [Accessed: 5 August 2012].

Alireza , I. and Vahideh, K. (2011) Does information technology affect the level of information literacy?: A comparative case study of high school students. *Aslib Proceedings*, 63 (6), p.618-631.

Blogger.com (2012) *Blog Stats-Overview*. [online] Available at: http://www.blogger.com/blogger.g?blogID=30050619362838527#overviewstats/src=dashboard [Accessed: 18 June 2012].

Bruce, C. (1999) Workplace experiences of information literacy. *International Journal of Information Management*, 19 (1999), p.33-47.

Careers360.com (2011) *Careers360-Yahoo! Distance Learning Survey 2011, Best Distance Learning institutes for the Top 10 Programmes*. [online] Available at: http://www.careers360.com/news/6538-Top-10-programmes-at-Best-DL-institute [Accessed: 23 August 2012].

Careers360.com (2011) *Careers360-Yahoo! Distance Learning Survey 2011, Careers360 - Yahoo! Perception survey of Distance Learning!*. [online] Available at: http://www.careers360.com/news/6525-Careers360-yahoo-distance-education-survey-2011 [Accessed: 23 August 2012].

Careers360.com (2011) *Careers360-Yahoo! Distance Learning Survey 2011, DL Institutes with best course material, study centres..more*. [online] Available at: http://www.careers360.com/news/6539-Top-10-DL-institutes-by-parameters [Accessed: 23 August 2012].

Careers360.com (2011) *Careers360-Yahoo! Distance Learning Survey 2011, India's Best Distance Learning Institutes 2011*. [online] Available at: http://www.careers360.com/news/6524-Best-Distance-Education-institute-2011 [Accessed: 23 August 2012].

Careers360.com (2011) *Careers360-Yahoo! Distance Learning Survey 2011, Students Ranking of Distance Learning Institutes*. [online] Available at: http://www.careers360.com/news/6536-Students-rate-the-best-distanceLearning-institutes [Accessed: 23 August 2012].

Distance Education Council (2012) *DEC Recognition Status of Universities/Institutions* . [online] Available at: http://www.dec.ac.in/PDF/Recogniton Status of SOUs & DEIs (Final).doc1.pdf [Accessed: 13 June 2012].

Elwood, J. and MacLean, G. (2009) ICT usage and student perceptions in Cambodia and Japan.*International Journal of Emerging Technologies and Society*, 7 (2), p.65-82.

Hamid, H. (2001) ICT risks widening of digital divide. *Business Times*, 29 March, p.07-07.

Jain, S. (2010) 40 Most Popular Social Networking Sites of the World. *Socialmediatoday*, [blog] 6 October 2010, Available at: http://socialmediatoday.com/soravjain/195917/40-most-popular-social-networking-sites-world [Accessed: 20 July 2012].

Lai, M. (2008) Technology readiness, internet self-efficacy and computing experience of professional accounting students. *Campus - Wide Information Systems*, 25 (1), p.18-29.

Marwaha, T. (n.p. – a) Feasibility study on using Social Media tools for enhancing interaction between students and IMT-CDL.

Marwaha, T. (n.p. – b) Studying the ICT Skills Level in students enrolled in IMT-CDL's Online Courses.

Musibau, A. et al. (2011) The implications of social networking sites in education in Nigeria. *Interdisciplinary Journal of Contemporary Research in Business*, 3 (7), p.93-101.

Mutula, S. (2002) ELearning initiative at the University of Botswana: Challenges and opportunities. *Campus - Wide Information Systems, 19(3)*, 99-99, 19 (3), p.99-109.

Parasuraman, A. (2000) Technology readiness index (TRI): A multiple-item scale to measure readiness to embrace new technologies. *Journal of Service Research: JSR*, 2 (4), p.307-320.

Pelgrin, W. (2009) Social Networking Sites: How To Stay Safe. *MS-ISAC Cyber Security Tips Newsletter*, 4 (3).

Prensky, M. (2001) Digital Natives, Digital Immigrants. *On the Horizon, MCB University Press*, 9 (5).

Rand, A. (1952) *The Fountainhead*. 50th Anniversary ed. New Jersey: Signet.

Salleh, M. et al. (2011) Measuring the Effect of Information Literacy on the Undergraduates' Academic Performance in Higher Education. *IPEDR*, 5 (2011), p.506-510.

Sen, T. (2011) Application of Blended and Traditional Class Teaching Approach in Higher Education and the Student Learning Experience. *International Journal of Innovation, Management and Technology*, 2 (2), p.107-109.

Skolnik, R. and Puzo, M. (2008) Utilization of laptop computers in the school of business classroom. *Academy of Educational Leadership Journal*, 12 (2), p.1-10.

TopTenReviews.com (2012) *Social Networking Websites Review 2012 - TopTenREVIEWS*. [online] Available at: http://social-networking-websites-review.toptenreviews.com/ [Accessed: 5 August 2012].

Westjohn, S. et al. (2009) Technology readiness and usage: A global-identity perspective. *Academy of Marketing Science*, 37 (3), p.250-265.

Learning Analytics Artefacts in a Cloud-Based Environment: A Design Science Perspective

Phelim Murnion[1] and Markus Helfert[2]

[1]School of Business, Galway-Mayo Institute of Technology, Galway, Ireland

[2]School of Computing, Dublin City University, Dublin, Ireland

Editorial Commentary

This case study explores the growing field of learning analytics, in the particular context of a group of business computing students in Higher Education in Ireland. Virtual learning environments and specific web-based or cloud-based technologies produce much data about learning and teaching activities which is generally under-used but has potential to improve the learning systems which generate the data. The research methodology in this case employs design science, looking at artefacts within a process: the development of a framework for learning analytics. This is a good example of a case study which is used not so much to test but to develop an innovation. By the convergence of a number of theories about the knowledge continuum, existing analytics models from business and models of learning and interaction, the authors have constructed a learning analytics framework with specific artefacts which can be applied to individual learner activities. This offers potential to intervene and improve or optimise the chances of learning improvement.

Abstract:: Learning analytics is the analysis of learning data for optimising learning and learning environments. A number of models or frameworks for learning analytics have been proposed, which focus on the process of analytics. Motivated by framework developments in other areas, such as systems development and IT management we propose to view learning analytics through the lens of design science. We identify a set of artefacts which extend the existing learning analytics framework along a second dimension. Incorporating a learning model based on interaction theory, the extended framework and artefacts are applied to a case study of business computing students studying customer relationship management in a cloud computing environment. The study shows the artefacts to be useful in extending the descriptive ability of the analytics framework. The significance of the work is that it provides a view of analytics through the lens of design science. In this way the extended framework provides a number of advantages for the application of learning analytics. The framework also contributes to learning analytics research by expanding the analytics vocabulary and providing tools for further research.

Keywords: learning analytics, business intelligence, cloud computing, design science

1. Introduction

Business Analytics is the practice of iterative, methodical exploration of an organization's data to support data-driven decision making (Barneveld, Arnold et al. 2012). Academic analytics is the application of this practice to education, responding to the reporting and decision making challenges facing academic leaders and managers (Oblinger and Campbell 2007). At the operational level of teaching and learning this can be applied as learning analytics, "the measurement, collection, analysis and reporting of data about learners and their contexts, for purposes of understanding and optimising learning and the environments in which it occurs" (SoLAR 2012).

Analytics is a process or methodology as well as a set of technologies. A number of models or frameworks for learning analytics have been proposed (Elias 2011). However, these frameworks are focussed on a single dimension of analytics: process. Frameworks in other similar problem domains are generally multi-dimensional, providing a number of different perspectives on a problem. Furthermore, analytical approaches are generally most successful when based on a clear model of the underlying problem domain. In education, E-learning theory describes a model of student learning, in which student activity and student interactions (with content and environment) are the primary drivers of learning.

Cloud computing services provide a novel information technology environment and are being widely deployed in education. Using the cloud, educators can now deploy sophisticated business applications such as SalesForce.com in the classroom, providing students with an immersive, real-life, active learning experience. Like the standard VLEs (such as Moodle), these systems offer an environment in which the user is immersed and user activity is extensively recorded. Furthermore, SalesForce, like many cloud systems, provides tools for accessing the database underlying the applications and for creating custom applications. This combination of rich data and technology tools presents an unique opportunity for the application of learning analytics.

The problem with current approaches is that they view learning analytics either from a technical point of view or a one-dimensional process view. In order to address this problem we apply a design science lens to investigate artefacts in Learning Analytics. In this paper, we introduce a set of learning analytics artefacts which modify existing Learning Analytics frameworks along a second dimension. The artefacts are designed using a design science approach and incorporating a learner interaction model. The artefacts are instantiated in a case study of computing students studying enterprise cloud computing. The main contribution of the paper is providing the set of artefacts and a modified framework that can assist researchers and practitioners to design, compare and validate learning analytics systems.

The remainder of the paper is structured as follows. In section two, we describe existing learning analytics frameworks. Following that we propose in section three a set of artefacts that modify the framework and relate the analytics framework to a learning model. Combining the modified analytics framework and the learning model, in section four we use a case study to examine the framework, followed by our conclusions.

2. Related work

2.1. Learning analytics

An increasingly complex environment, a vast proliferation of data, and greater competition, has forced organisations to use information technologies as a platform for a more analytical approach to management and decision making (Hopkins, Kruschwitz et al. 2010). Variously described as business intelligence, business analytics, or data mining and knowledge discovery, this approach has become a major trend in the application of information technologies to organisational management (Hostmann, Rayner et al. 2006).

Within educational technology, there has been a recent expansion of analytical approaches such as educational data mining (Romero and Ventura 2010) and academic analytics (Barneveld, Arnold et al. 2012). However, much of the analytics research has been at the institutional level (Hopkins, Kruschwitz et al. 2010), (Oblinger and Campbell 2007), rather than the level of individual learners and educators and these approaches have not as yet been widely applied to cloud-based environments. Furthermore, the analytics approaches tested so far have tended to focus on technical aspects of analytics and have been insufficiently integrated with the practice of teaching and learning or with the wider field of educational technology research (Baker and Yacef 2009), (Murnion and Helfert 2011). Experience in applications of analytics has indicated that analytics is most successful when applied using a framework or model that guides the analytics process and relates that process to the underlying problem domain (Shearer 2000).

2.2. Analytics frameworks and methodologies

A number of models for business analytics have been described: (Shearer 2000), (Hostmann, Rayner et al. 2006), (Oblinger and Campbell 2007), (Hopkins, Kruschwitz et al. 2010), (Elias 2011), Selecting the more recent analytics models that describe the process of analytics, it is clear that they share a number of common elements, as shown in table 1 below.

Table 1: Analytics models and elements

Analytics Model (Oblinger and Campbell 2007)	IBM Analytics Model (Hopkins, Kruschwitz et al. 2010)	Learning Analytics Model (Elias 2011)
Capture	Define	Select & Capture
Report	Capture	Aggregate & Report
Predict	Aggregate	Predict
Act/Share	Analyze	Use
Refine	Disseminate	Refine
		Share

From the above sample it can be seen that there is general agreement on the required elements of an analytics process. These can be summarised as: capture & organise, aggregate & report, predict, act/share, and refine.

2.2.1. Capture & Organise

Data is the basis of all analytics techniques. However, the definition of the data to captured can be problematic (Hopkins, Kruschwitz et al. 2010), (Elias 2011). The data can be required from multiple different sources (Oblinger and Campbell 2007) and must be captured, organised and stored using appropriate data management or data warehousing tools (Hoffer, Prescott et al. 2007). Too often, this process can consume too much of the analytics effort (Hopkins, Kruschwitz et al. 2010).

2.2.2. Aggregate & Report

The organised data can be summarised and aggregated into reports containing descriptive, meaningful information, although text-based reports are increasingly being replaced by graphical dashboards and complex visualisation methods (Mazza and Milani 2004). Reporting involves decisions about key metrics to be measured and displayed (Rogers, McEwen et al. 2010) and the deployment of query and descriptive statistics tools (Oblinger and Campbell 2007)

2.3. Predict

The aggregated data can be analyzed using statistical methods. Key factors in the success if this process are the effectiveness of the predictive models selected and the skills of the analytics team (Oblinger and Campbell 2007). A typical application in learning analytics is predicting final student grades from course data (Macfadyen and Dawson 2010). Prediction is usually based on statistical algorithms such as regression models. Timing and frequency of model operations depends on the problem being solved (Oblinger and Campbell 2007).

2.3.1. Act/Share

A key feature of successful analytics is ensuring that the analysis is actionable (Norris, Baer et al. 2008). Action can range across a spectrum from simple information provision for decision makers to triggers to educational interventions (Oblinger and Campbell 2007). In many cases, the action can be to share the knowledge created in a collaborative decision making environment (Dron and Anderson 2009).

2.3.2. Refine

Analytics approaches should include a self-improvement process, periodically amending models and methods (Oblinger and Campbell 2007), returning results of the analysis in a feedback loop improving the learning system (Romero and Ventura 2007), and at its best, embedding the results of analytics into the decision making processes (Hopkins, Kruschwitz et al. 2010).

However, despite the general consensus on elements of the analytics framework, it is quite sparse in that only one dimension is described: the set of methods (a process dimension). Analytics is both a methodology and a complex technical process. Other information systems-based methodologies and processes of similar scale have been described from multiple different perspectives. For example, the development process for large information systems, the Systems Development Life Cycle (SDLC) has been described from a multitude of perspectives or dimensions; from phases and processes to models and structures (Whitten, Bentley et al. 1998). Similarly, the management of IT systems in organisations has been described by frameworks which are multi-dimensional such as the Zachman framework (Zachman 1987) and the IT-CMF framework (Curley 2009).

This approach, of describing a set of dimensions for a framework, requires a design methodology. One such methodology is Design science, a research methodology that aims to use the design of artefacts (which may be frameworks, models, or methods) as the central component of research (Carcary 2011). In order to investigate artefacts of learning analytics, we employ a design science perspective.

3. Design science and framework development

Design science is a research methodology that is centred on the production of artefacts that can be evaluated for practical utility and for contribution to theory (Hevner, March et al. 2004). Design science takes as its fundamental building blocks four types of artefacts (March and Smith 1995). **Constructs** are concepts which form the vocabulary of the research problem. **Methods** are steps (or guidelines) used to complete a task, and based on the underlying constructs. **Models** are representations of the problems area, describing how things are. **Instantiations** are the realisation of an artefact in its environment. For this study design science provides a lens with which to view the problem of learning analytics frameworks and a vocabulary to describe the process of framework development.

Based on this understanding, the first requirement is identification of a common vocabulary; in design science terms the requisite *constructs*. Several descriptions of analytics approaches have referred to the concept of the knowledge continuum (Elias 2011), (Romero and Ventura 2007), (Murnion and Lally 2009), in which data at the bottom of the continuum is converted into information, then knowledge and then wisdom. The continuum is often depicted as a knowledge pyramid (Ackoff 1989). In her examination of analytics frameworks, Elias (2011) matched the elements of the knowledge continuum to the processes of analytics.

Table 2: Knowledge continuum of analytics (Elias 2011)

Knowledge Continuum (Constructs)		Steps of Analytics (Methods)
Data	Obtain Raw Facts	Capture
Information	Give Meaning to Obtained Data	Report
Knowledge	Analyze and Synthesize Derived Information	Predict
Wisdom	Use Knowledge to Establish and Achieve Goals	Act
		Refine

Given a set of *constructs* which form the basis of the analytics framework and a set of *methods* for progressing through the framework, we propose another perspective on analytics (in the vocabulary of Design Science, a set of artefacts) which is a set of *models* providing representations of the analytics problem for each method.

3.1. Proposed analytics artefacts

Based on the fundamental construct, the knowledge continuum, we propose and describe new artefacts, specifically analytics models, one for each analytics method.

Table 3: Analytics artefacts

Methods	Models (Artefacts)
Capture	Data model
Report	Information model
Predict	Predictive model
Act	Decision model
Refine	Analytics model

3.1.1. Data model

A data model provides a representation of the existing data in the source data system(s). These can be described using standard database models (such as entity-relationship diagram models)

3.1.2. Information model

Describes the information for reports, including simple aggregation functions such as Sum() and Count() and more complex models such as cross-tabulations. In addition to describing the precise content and structure of the information an information model could also include descriptions of the type of information required. An example would be information quality metrics such as timeliness, accuracy, and completeness (Alkhattabi, Neagu et al. 2010).

3.1.3. Predictive Model

There are libraries of standard predictive models (regression, classification, association, etc.). However the analytics prediction model might incorporate further factors such as model reliability and timing of model runs (Oblinger and Campbell 2007).

3.1.4. Decision Model

A decision model can be as simple as directing relevant information to appropriate decision makers at the right time i.e. a reporting rules system, in contrast to the information model which deals with the content of reports. A more complex decision model could trigger actions based on a rule-base consisting of a set of IF ... THEN rules or a formal decision tree. However production rules and decision trees are mostly suited to highly structured, routine decisions. More sophisticated decision models could incorporate elements of the decision making process such as support for collaborative decision making.

3.1.5. Analytics model

For analytics to improve (Refine method), the analytics methods themselves must be modelled within the system. This meta-model could be as simple as the set of the other four models plus model management meta-data e.g. model creation data, model execution data, user comments, etc. However if the Refine method is to impact on the underlying learning (rather than only on the analytics) the analytics model should include a model of the learning context.

Using Design science as a lens to view the problem, we have amended the existing framework by adding new artefacts, a set of models. The fourth artefact type in design science, *instantiation*, refers to the realisation of the other artefacts in their environment. In order to do this it is necessary to relate each artefact to the underlying domain of teaching and learning. That requires another construct: a learning model.

3.2. Learning model and interaction

In order for analytics to be effective, an understanding of the domain to be analysed is required, whether that is to generate a problem definition (Shearer 2000), provide a basis for the general design of the analytics system (Pahl 2006), or to determine the precise data that needs to be captured for analysis (Oblinger and Campbell 2007). One way to understand this domain is to use an accepted learning model.

One of the central features of learning is learner interaction (Anderson 2008), (Ohl 2001). Interaction can be of three types: learner - content, learner - interface and learner – support (Moore 1989). Computer-based learning environments which simulate a real-life system can provide a particularly effective learner – content interaction (Ohl 2001). These kinds of learning environments support activity based learning, the acquisition of knowledge by actions, or operations (Ohl 2001). Learner activities, such as application and practice, generate interactions with learning content, which in return generate new activities (Ally 2008).

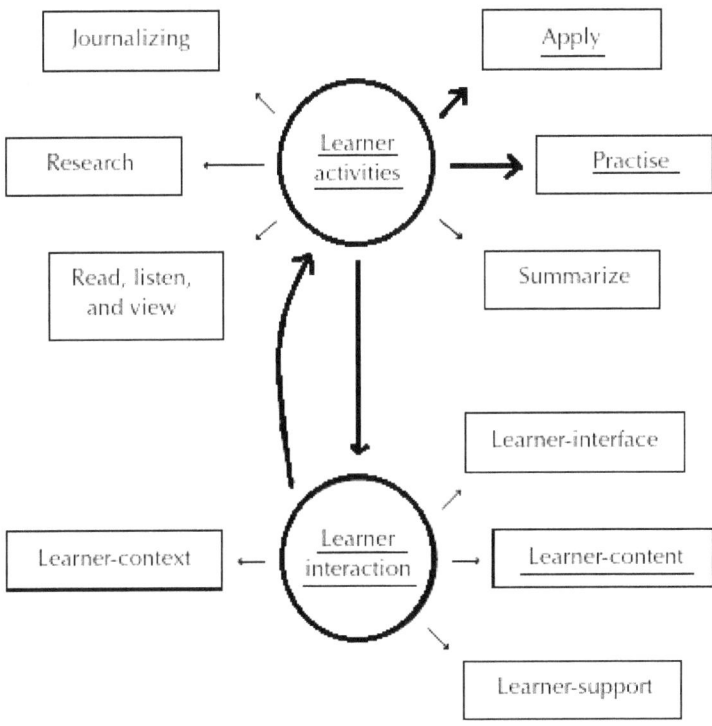

Figure 1: Learning Model (from (Ally 2008), our emphases)

Based on the model described above we propose that in a computer-based active learning environment **learner – content** interaction is critical and that this interaction, in an applied learning context, requires and causes continuous student activity in the form of **application** and **practice**.

However learner – content interaction is not simply a one-dimensional scalar variable, it is a multi-faceted concept (Anderson 2008). Much educational practice assumes this uni-dimensionality, for example counting student attendance. Several applications of analytics to online learning, similarly, use a count of student logins as a measure of student activity, such as the usage statistics in Moodle reports (www.moodle.org), or studies measuring LMS usage (Heathcote and Dawson 2005). However other researchers have defined measures of interaction which are qualitative (Janossy 2008) and multi-dimensional (Roblyer and Ekhaml 2000). The extensive field of educational data mining (EDM) is predicated on the principal that learner interactions, or learner behaviour, involves complex patterns amenable to data mining algorithmic approaches (Baker and Yacef 2009), (Romero and Ventura 2010). Thus, an understanding of learner activities and learner – content interactions provides not only the basis for the simplest artefact, the Data model, but also for the more complex artefacts such as the Information and Predictive models. In section 4 we combine this interaction-based learning model with our proposed analytics artefacts in a case study of learning analytics in a cloud computing environment.

4. The case study

4.1. The context: Cloud-based services for business computing education

The case study is based on the students in first year of a Business Computing degree. The students use a cloud computing system for customer relationship management (CRM).

Cloud computing is the provision of simple, on-demand access to pools of highly elastic computing resources as a service over the Internet, where the user need not be concerned about how it works it, or where it is located (Marks and Lozano 2010). Cloud computing can be divided into several service layers: The final layer; Software as a Service (SaaS), is what users and consumers of cloud computing interact with, when they access their Google docs or upload images to a photo sharing application online. With SaaS the user is getting a complete information system or application suite, but as a service, rather than as purchased software installed on a local machine. One of the most well-known and established SaaS providers is Salesforce.com, the "enterprise cloud computing company" (www.salesforce.com). Salesforce.com now offers a raft of cloud computing solutions, but it's original and most well-known service is the customer relationship management (CRM) service now called Sales Cloud but still known as Salesforce by the user community.

CRM is a set of business processes and related technologies for managing customer relationships to add value for customers and thereby the company (Chalmeta 2006). CRM technologies evolved from contact managers and sales force automation tools into complete systems that manage customer relationships in a single way and provide an integrated view of customers. As such, CRM is a central element of the marketing function (Kumar and Reinartz 2006). Business computing students using the Salesforce CRM system are thus able to interact with the customer life cycle (Berry and Linoff 2011) and are also exposed to enterprise-level cloud computing technology.

Using this technology, it is possible to create an effective learning environment for business computing students. In terms of the learning model from section 3.2, the emphasis is very much on Learner – Content interaction. Students are assigned typical tasks associated with the customer lifecycle: creating new Leads, converting Leads into Contacts and Accounts, and updating Opportunities. Because the system contains a central database, each student sees the activity of all the other students. At the same time, because Salesforce is designed to create a collaborative work environment, each piece of newly created data is assigned an owner, so each student can identify exactly what data belongs to them. As the students work through the customer lifecycle they continuously update the CRM database which provides a detailed source of student activity data for learning analytics. In the next section we describe examples of learning analytics artefacts derived during the case study.

4.2. Case/implementation

The Business Computing students worked in the Salesforce CRM environment for part of a semester and were examined on Salesforce and CRM element at the end of that period. The data was extracted from Salesforce using the Force.com Explorer and the Salesforce Object Query Language (SOQL). The information modals were created and stored in a data warehouse created with Microsoft Access 2007 and further analytical models were constructed using the IBM SPSS Modeller suite.. In our complete case study we constructed a number of analytics scenarios, each of which described a complete instance of the Learning Analytics framework. However due to space constraints we present here only one scenario.

4.2.1. Scenario

In this scenario the objective of the analytics process is to examine a particular pattern of learner activity. In this learning context, which is activity-based and applied, application and practice are the key to learner – content interaction and thus effective learning. We assume that the total amount of interaction is less important than continuity of interaction. The analytical hypothesis is that a gap in activity will be detrimental to learning outcomes. Based on this analytical problem we can define the appropriate analytics artefacts.

Table 2: Scenario examples

Artifact	Description	Example (highly summarized for illustrative purposes)
Data model		
	The required data is a count of specific activities, for each user, with a date stamp for each activity, from the Sales force database. Also final student grades from the examiner. The two data sets are joined on student ID.	Activity data ID Activity Date 01 Create Lead 02/03 Student grades 03 Create Lead 02/03 ID Grade 01 Create Lead 08/03 01 67 : : : 02 36: :
Information model		
	The model groups activity data into time periods (weeks) by user. Activity in a time period is given a binary classification: 0 if zero learner activity, 1 if learner activity is greater than zero. Finally the number of non-zero time periods is counted. Final grades are converted into a binary Pass(1)/Fail(0) Grade	Activity Learner Wk1 Wk2 Wk3 Non-zeros 01 1 1 0 2 02 1 0 0 1 : : : : : 27 1 0 1 2 Student Grades ID Grade 01 1 : : : 02 2

Artifact	Description	Example (highly summarized for illustrative purposes)
Predictive model		
	A Classification model is used. Learners are classified as Pass/Fail based on activity aggregate (non-zeros) in the information model	The model used was Chi-square. The results were statistically significant ($p = 0.047$) suggesting that gaps in student activity deserved some action
Decision model		
	Timing of analysis is necessarily end of module since final grades were used. Decision rule can be to amend next run of module	Based on the findings of the predictive model a possible solution is to insert continuous assessment.
Analytics Process model		
	The Salesforce setup includes a dashboard for the administrator (Tutor) showing raw student activity data. The predictive model provides greater analytical insight than this data.	Refine the system by adding the results of the information model (summarised) to the dashboard.

From the scenario described we can see the complete learning analytics framework in action including instances of each of the learning analytics artefacts, albeit in a highly summarised form. An important feature of artefacts in design science is that they are observable and measurable and thus contribute to the general theory or framework. This case shows how each artefact can be instantiated and described in concrete terms. In the next section we make some conclusions based on this work.

5. Conclusion and further research

Our framework extends existing analytics frameworks by viewing learning analytics through the lens of design science, which allows us to identify relevant artefacts. We introduced and described learning analytics artefacts in the form of a set of models that relate existing analytics methods to the underlying construct, the data-knowledge continuum. Based on the case study we were able to observe and describe the implementation of the extended framework and the new artefacts. The new framework makes a number of contributions. Existing analytics frameworks have been focussed on the process (methods) of moving up the knowledge continuum, from data to knowledge. The addition of the new artefacts provides a different, descriptive perspective, allowing analysts to check and describe exactly where they are on the knowledge continuum at any point in the process. Furthermore, these models by their nature consist of persistent data that can be stored and shared. Sharing can occur along the time dimension so that the goal of continuously improving and refining the analytics process can be more easily achieved. Sharing can also occur on the organisational dimension, where models developed in one analytics process can be shared and re-used in other parallel analytics attempts. The framework also attempts to address the perennial requirement of analytics to be connected to the underlying problem domain. The particular learning model used in our case might not be universally accepted but we expect that the process of relating knowledge artefacts in an analytics process to a learning model should always occur in an effective learning analytics approach. In addition to these advantages in the application of learning analytics we expect that our framework will make a contribution to learning analytics research. The artefacts we have described and instantiated are concrete, observable and measurable, expanding the vocabulary of learning analytics and providing tools for further research. Furthermore the paper contributes to Design science research by demonstrating how Design science can be employed to analyse a complex information technology application environment, such as learning analytics.

Based on this work we see a number of further research directions. The first is the possibility of identifying further artefact sets (dimensions) to be described and tested. We have extended the framework by adding a models dimension to the existing methods dimension. There could be other dimensions to analytics that require examination, for example a technology dimension, describing the Information technology tools and systems being used and connected to at each stage in the analytics process. Finally we identify a limitation in applying Design science to identify artefacts. So far we have only observed and structured the set of artefacts. In further research we aim to complete the design of these models

References

Ackoff, R. L. (1989). "From Data to Wisdom." Journal of Applies Systems Analysis **16**: 3-9.

Alkhattabi, M., D. Neagu, et al. (2010). "Information Quality Framework for e-Learning Systems." Knowledge Management & E-Learning: An International Journal **2**(4).

Ally, M. (2008). Foundations of Educational Theory for Online Learning. The Theory and Practice of Online Learning, AU Press: 15-44.

Anderson, T. (2008). Towards a Theory of Online Learning. The Theory and Practice of Online Learning. T. Anderson, AU Press: 45-74.

Baker, R. and K. Yacef (2009). "The State of Educational Data Mining in 2009: A Review and Future Visions." Journal of Educational Data Mining **1**(1): 3-17.

Barneveld, A. v., K. Arnold, et al. (2012). Analytics in Higher Education: Establishing a Common Language. EDUCAUSE Learning Initiative, EDUCAUSE.

Berry, M. J. A. and G. S. Linoff (2011). Data Mining Techniques : For Marketing, Sales, and Customer Relationship Management. Hoboken, NJ, USA, John Wiley & Sons, Incorporated.

Carcary, M. (2011). "Design Science Research: The Case of the IT Capability Maturity Framework (IT CMF)." The Electronic Journal of Business Research Methods **9**(2): 109-118.

Chalmeta, R. (2006). "Methodology for customer relationship management." The Journal of Systems and Software **79**: 1015-1024.

Curley, M. (2009). Introducing an IT Capability Maturity Framework. Enterprise Information Systems. **12**: 63-78.

Dron, J. and T. Anderson (2009). On the design of collective applications. Proceedings of the 2009 International Conference on Computational Science and Engineering ,.

Elias, T. (2011). Learning Analytics: Definitions, Processes and Potential, Learning and Knowledge Analytics.

Heathcote, E. and S. Dawson (2005). Data Mining for Evaluation, Benchmarking and Reflective Practice in a LMS. World Conference on E-Learning in Corporate, Government, Healthcare, and Higher Education (ELEARN). Chesapeake, VA.

Hevner, A., S. March, et al. (2004). "Design Science Research in Information Systems." MIS Quarterly **28**(1): 75-105.

Hoffer, J. A., M. Prescott, et al. (2007). Modern Database Management, 8/e. NJ, Prentice Hall.

Hopkins, M. S., N. Kruschwitz, et al. (2010). Analytics: The New Path to Value MITSloan Management Review.

Hostmann, B., N. Rayner, et al. (2006). Gartner's Business Intelligence, Analytics and Performance Management Framework. 2009. Stamford, Gartner.

Janossy, J. H., T. (2008). Proposed Model for Evaluating C/LMS Faculty Usage in Higher Education Institutions. Society for Information Technology & Teacher Education International Conference, Las Vegas, Nevada, USA.

Kumar, V. and W. J. Reinartz (2006). Customer relationship management: a databased approach, Wiley.

Macfadyen, L. P. and S. Dawson (2010). "Mining LMS data to develop an "early warning system" for educators: A proof of concept." Computers & education: 588-599.

March, S. T. and G. F. Smith (1995). "Design and natural science research on information technology." Decision Support Systems **15**(4): 251-266.

Marks, E. A. and B. Lozano (2010). Cloud Computing. NJ, USA, Wiley.

Mazza, R. and C. Milani (2004). GISMO: A graphical interactive student monitoring tool for course management systems. Int. Conf. Technol. Enhanced Learn. Milan, Italy: 1-8.

Moore, M. G. (1989). "Three types of interaction." The American Journal of Distance Education **3**(2): 1-6.

Murnion, P. and M. Helfert (2011). A Framework for Decision Support for Learning Management Systems. 10th European Conference on e-Learning ECEL-2011. Brighton, UK.

Murnion, P. and C. Lally (2009). The Development and Validation of Data Transformation Functions in Educational Assessment Data. Information Systems Development: Challeneges in Practice, theory, and Education. C. B. e. al., Springer. **2**.

Norris, D., L. Baer, et al. (2008). "Action Analytics: Measuring and Improving Performance That Matters in Higher Education." EDUCAUSE Review **43**(1): 42-67.

Oblinger, D. G. and J. P. Campbell (2007). Academic Analytics, EDUCAUSE.

Ohl, T. M. (2001). "An Interaction-Centric Learning Model." Journal of Educational Multimedia and Hypermedia **10**(4): 311-332.

Pahl, C. (2006). Data Mining for the Analysis of Content Interaction in Web-based Learning and Training Systems. Data Mining in E-Learning, WIT Press: 41-56.

Roblyer, M. D. and L. Ekhaml (2000). "How interactive are YOUR distance courses? A rubric for assessing interaction in distance learning." Online Journal of Distance Learning Administration **3**(2).

Rogers, P. C., M. R. McEwen, et al. (2010). The design and evaluation of distance education. Emerging technologies in distance education. G. Veletsianos: 231-247.

Romero, C. and S. Ventura (2007). "Educational data mining: A survey from 1995 to 2005." Expert Systems with Applications(33): 135-146.

Romero, C. and S. Ventura (2010). "Educational Data Mining: A Review of the State of the Art." IEEE TRANSACTIONS ON SYSTEMS, MAN, AND CYBERNETICS—PART C: APPLICATIONS AND REVIEWS **40**(6): 601-618.

Shearer, C. (2000). "The CRISP-DM model: The new blueprint for data mining." Journal of Data Warehousing **5**(4).

SoLAR. (2012). "Solar: Society for Learning Analytics Research." Retrieved 15/05/2012, 2011, from http://www.solaresearch.org/mission/about/.

Whitten, J. L., L. D. Bentley, et al. (1998). Systems analysis and design methods, Irwin/McGraw-Hill.

Zachman, J. A. (1987). "A framework for information systems architecture " IBM Systems Journal **26**(3): 276-292.

eLearning: Tool to Ensure Growth and Sustainability of SMEs

Andrée Roy
Université de Moncton, Moncton, Canada

Editorial Commentary

Positioning learning as an engine for business growth and survival, this Canadian case study tackles the challenge of introducing eLearning to Small and Medium Sized Enterprises. Although there is plenty of literature extolling the resource arguments for eLearning and the vital need for business learning in order to stay ahead in dynamic and highly competitive markets, actually convincing SMEs of 500 employees or fewer to adopt eLearning strategies remains a difficult task. Multiple case studies are used here, to move forward on the basis of a literature review which proposes a range of positive benefits from eLearning for SMEs. The key limiting factors appear to be a lack of appreciation of the value of learning in SMEs, as well as lack of awareness of the nature and positive advantages of eLearning. It may be that SMEs are unable to make these changes on their own, and need the help of Government agencies to spread the word.

Abstract: This study makes a census of the written material on how eLearning can help businesses ensure their growth and their sustainability. A multiple case study shows that SMEs in Atlantic Canada find that benefits they get from eLearning, such as the reduction of the total training cost, and the possibility for the learner and for the business to choose the time and the location of the course, can help them ensure their growth and their sustainability. Some of the other factors they find that can help them ensure their growth and their sustainability include the possibility for the learner to only complete the part of the course that pertains to his needs rather than the entire course, the possibility for each learner to learn at his own pace and the possibility of evaluating the progress of the learners on a continuous basis. This study also proposes a plan to help the different actors of economic development introduce eLearning to SMEs.

Keywords: benefits of eLearning, eLearning, growth, SMEs, sustainability

1. Introduction

A company's investment in the training and the updating of their employees' skills is a key element of growth in the knowledge-based economies. Organizations and businesses including small and medium-sized enterprises (SMEs) need to exploit the benefits associated with eLearning in order to address their training needs, and to ensure their growth and their survival.

Indeed, if companies want to position themselves so that they can compete on a global scale, they will need better skilled employees, and in order to achieve this, they will need to embark on a cultural change towards training. Moreover, the cultural change must be transmitted and be adopted by all stakeholders, i.e. by SMEs, the various players in economic development and society in general. ELearning has to be part of their development in order to ensure their sustainability.

In Atlantic Canada, SMEs, which are defined as businesses having fewer than 500 employees, represent the majority of businesses, and they also create the majority of jobs (APECA 1998). Due to their great flexibility and their adaptability, they represent the sector of the economy that creates the most employment (APECA 2005; Brady 1995), and has the greatest growth rate. They are considered the foundation of economic development (APECA 2005; Mittelstaedt, Harben and Ward 2003; Roffe 2007). Therefore, it is important to know if eLearning can help SMEs ensure their growth and their sustainability because capability development of small firms in Atlantic Canada like in other parts of the world remains critical to economic prosperity (see for example Matlay 1999; APECA 2005; Jayawarna & al. 2007; Roffe 2007).

The purpose of this study is two-fold. After having identified how eLearning can help businesses to ensure their growth and their sustainability, based on a survey of the documentation on the issue, the first objective is to determine through a case study if the SMEs in Atlantic Canada find that eLearning can help them to ensure their growth and their sustainability. If so, the second step is presenting a plan to help the different actors of economic development to introduce eLearning to SMEs.

Thus, the remainder of the document is arranged as follows: Section 2 presents the method used for the article. Section 3 presents a literature census on how eLearning can help businesses to ensure their growth and their sustainability. Section 4 presents, through a case study, the extent to which Atlantic Canadian SMEs find that eLearning can help them to ensure their growth and their sustainability. It also proposes a plan to help the different actors of economic development introduce eLearning to SMEs. The conclusion and discussion will be included in section 5.

2. Method

Given the present state of knowledge on eLearning in SMEs, the method used for this article includes a census of the literature on eLearning combined with qualitative and exploratory research approach, i.e. multiple case studies. The literature census covers more specifically how eLearning can help businesses ensure their growth and their sustainability. The case study method is well adapted in situations where theoretical propositions are few and where field experience is still limited (Yin 1994). A multiple-site case study allows one to understand the particular context and the evolution of each firm with regard to eLearning. Sixteen SMEs located in the Atlantic Region of Canada were studied: four in New Brunswick, four in Nova Scotia, four in Prince Edward Island and four in Newfoundland, selected to be sufficiently successful (at least 10 years in business) and representative in terms of industry and size, for theoretical generalization purposes. These manufacturing SMEs stem from various sectors such as: textile, oil and gas, pulp and paper, and processed food. Following North American research (Mittelstaedt, Harben and Ward 2003; Wolff and Pett 2000), a small enterprise (SE) is defined as having 20 to 99 employees, whereas a medium-sized enterprise (ME) has 100 to 499.

Data were collected through semi-structured tape-recorded interviews ranging approximately two hours each with the owner-manager or CEO and with the firm's HR manager or manager responsible for training. eLearning users were also interviewed in four cases. The interviews were conducted based on a pre-tested questionnaire and transcript. Interview transcripts were then coded and analyzed following Miles and Huberman's (1994) prescriptions with the assistance of the Atlas.ti application. For reasons of confidentiality, fictitious names were used to refer to the individuals and the firms participating in the study. As presented in the research results section, these firms range in size from 60 to 485 employees, and operate in industries where the technological intensity varies from low to high. All export except for one firm (M). The SMEs were regrouped in four eLearning profiles of increasing intensity based on the extent of their awareness and their use of eLearning (none, weak, average, strong).

3. Literature census

Several organizations are faced with the need to produce learning at a faster pace in order to gain and to sustain competitive advantage (Taran 2006). The recent technological advances along with a reduction of their costs allow them to do so with eLearning. Indeed eLearning is closely associated with many benefits that can help organizations and businesses, including SMEs, to achieve a competitive advantage and to ensure their growth and their sustainability

As mentioned, eLearning can bring a large number of benefits to several organizations and businesses. For example, eLearning offers businesses the potential to provide flexible, accessible and supportive learning since learners can gain access from any locations at times convenient to both the learner and the employer. It can also create value, reduce costs, save time, give fast feedback, or achieve a combination of all that address efficiency issues. On this issue, Tyler (2001) indicates that eLearning can be beneficial to SMEs for various reasons. The reasons he specifies include that it allows saving on travel costs, that it ensures that the training needs can be filled at a more appropriate time for the SMEs and for the individuals in these SMEs, and that it allows to avoid having to replace employees during work hours. Rosenberg (2002) mentions that eLearning provides a higher retention rate and a faster distribution of the training material while ensuring a consistent delivery of the course's content compared to a professor. As for Pantaziz (2002), he mentions that eLearning reduces the training time and can increase productivity and prosperity of the business and the individuals. In his opinion, the benefits of eLearning are based on the dynamic relationship between learning, the individuals and the performance of the organisation along with the access to quality training at just the right time. Another benefit, not the least, learners seem to agree that they can gain extra knowledge that will improve their career advancement and learn new technological skills (Baldwin-Evans 2004; Homan and Macpherson 2005; Willging and Johnson 2004).

The various benefits of eLearning that can help businesses to ensure their growth and their sustainability have been reported extensively and can be broadly classified as shown in Table 1.

Table 1: Benefits of eLearning

Benefits	Explanation
Flexibility and accessibility	The possibility for the learner and for the business to choose the time (any time – 24 hours a day / 7 days per week) and the location (anywhere – any geographic location) where the course is taken. (Baldwin-Evans 2004; Kenyon 2002; Melymuka 2002; Nonprofit World 2002; Perez and Foshay 2002; Rosenberg 2002; Sloman 2001).
Modularity	The possibility for the learner to only complete the part of the course that pertains to his needs rather than the entire course (Melymuka 2002) along with the possibility of working on the sections that are not understood as well (Youngers 2002).
Learning pace	The possibility for each learner to learn at his or her own pace (Nonprofit World 2002; Perez and Foshay 2002).
Privacy	The possibility of completing the course alone at home (privacy) and not having to suffer the discomforts (shyness, feeling of lack of knowledge, ...) that some learners experience from time to time (Perez and Foshay 2002).

Benefits	Explanation
Interactive Feedback	The possibility of having a teacher and personalised support by an instructor, and the possibility of getting feedback from various means (telephone, fax, e-mail, camera ...) (Melymuka 2002; Perez and Foshay 2002).
Cost effective	The reduction of the total training costs (course, transportation, meals, lodging, time away from work). There are numerous courses already developed in the e-earning format that are free or available at very reasonable prices. These courses, in addition to being less expensive than conventional courses, allow the SMEs to save on travel time, money, lodging and meal costs. These courses avoid the loss of production time or the need to replace production time for a business. (Kenyon 2002; Melymuka 2002; Pantaziz 2002; Rosenberg 2002; Youngers 2002).
Learning style	The possibility of presenting the course material in various formats (selection of a variety of activities) and of meeting the various learning styles of the learners (Melymuka 2002; Young 2002).
Customisation	The possibility of customising the learning according to everyone's needs. For example, the possibility to select learning materials that meet the learners' level of knowledge, interest and what they need to know to perform more effectively at/in/doing their job (Sloman 2001; Youngers 2002; Zahner 2002).
Evaluation	The possibility of evaluating the progress of the learners on a continuous basis (Kenyon 2002; Youngers 2002).
Distribution of literature	A faster distribution of the training material (Rosenberg 2002).
Consistent delivery	A consistent delivery of the content of the course compared to a professor (EIU 2004; Halkett 2002; Rosenberg 2002).

Several surveys performed with businesses confirm these benefits. For example, according to a first survey, businesses believe that the two main benefits of eLearning are its capacity to be accessed in the workplace, thus reducing the time spent outside the work area, and its capacity to structure the training in small modules that will meet the training needs of the learners. As for the employees, they believe the benefits of eLearning are its convenience and the opportunity to learn at one's own pace (Industrial and Commercial Training 2001). According to another survey, the majority of businesses believe that eLearning is an economical, efficient, flexible, practical and time-effective mean of training that reduces the training time of employees (Journal of European Industrial Training 2002).

eLearning offers many advantages for businesses. It is now necessary to verify, through a case study, if Atlantic Canadian SMEs find that eLearning can help ensure their growth and their sustainability.

4. Research results

The study shows that the majority of SMEs use eLearning in order to offer training to their employees and to increase their growth and their sustainability. However, as shown in table 2, some SMEs do not use it at all. A detailed study also provides for categorizing SMEs into four distinct profiles of eLearning users. There are SMEs that use eLearning a lot (strong use), those that use it quite a bit (average use), those that only use it a little bit (weak use), and those that don't use it at all (non-existent use) as indicated in Table 2[1].

Table 3 also shows that several SMEs in Atlantic Canada use eLearning to train their employees. During this study, 75% of SMEs were using eLearning to train their employees. This tends to confirm what Bassi and Van Buren (1999) indicate, i.e. that Internet and Web-based training methods are being increasingly used by SMEs. An interesting fact to note in the case of a "weak" use of eLearning by

---

[1] Note: In Table 3, a "strong" use means that the business regularly uses eLearning to train its employees. An "average" use means that the business has developed at least two courses in eLearning format and that the production employees must take these courses. A "weak" use means that only a few employees use it in the business and a "non-existent" use means that the business does not use eLearning to train its employees and that they do not use it to develop their knowledge.

SMEs is that it is usually the employee who has chosen to develop his/her knowledge through eLearning. Julien (firm J) provides an example *"Some employees have chosen eLearning, but it is usually on an exception basis, to develop their work knowledge and it was suggested by the employee and not the employer"*.

Table 2: Profiles of eLearning's utilization by SMEs

	Profile I STRONG (C, D, K, L)	Profile II average (B, E, M, O)	Profile III WEAK (A, F, I, J)	Profile IV non-existent (G, H, N, P)
Size				
Number of employees	300 to 485	60 to 280	150 to 350	75 to 400
ELearning				
Utilization	strong	average	weak	non-existent

Table 3 also shows that several SMEs in Atlantic Canada use eLearning to train their employees. During this study, 75% of SMEs were using eLearning to train their employees. This tends to confirm what Bassi and Van Buren (1999) indicate, i.e. that Internet and Web-based training methods are being increasingly used by SMEs. An interesting fact to note in the case of a "weak" use of eLearning by SMEs is that it is usually the employee who has chosen to develop his/her knowledge through eLearning. Julien (firm J) provides an example *"Some employees have chosen eLearning, but it is usually on an exception basis, to develop their work knowledge and it was suggested by the employee and not the employer"*.

The decision to use eLearning by the employees in order to further develop their knowledge is linked to their perceived benefits of eLearning. Fiona (F) provides us with an example: *"The employee chose this method because she wanted to continue working; she needs to work; she wanted to complete her bachelor's degree while working at the same time"*. Denise (D) gives us another example: *"Since I have a three year-old daughter and that my work schedule is rather full, I can complete the work at 3:00 am in my slippers. Honestly, I chose eLearning because of the flexibility"*. As for SMEs' choice to use eLearning to train their employees, that decision is also a function of the benefits they may obtain from eLearning. To this effect, Table 3 illustrates different statements regarding the perceived benefits of eLearning by SMEs who use it. These benefits are basically the same as those described in the literature. These benefits, as shown in Table 4, are not only perceived benefits, but attainable benefits that motivate SMEs to further use eLearning for training purposes and to ensure their growth and their sustainability.

Table 3: Benefits of eLearning as perceived by SMEs

Benefits	Explanation of the benefits
Cost	Cost reductions (course, travel, lost time) (Arthur, A; Ivan, I; Marie, M).
	It is training that is not costly when you only have 1 or 2 people to train, as it is not necessary to hire a trainer (Bert, B; Karen, K).
	It is an efficient way, cost-wise, to offer training. It reduces travel and meal costs [...] and reduces the time lost from work (Marie, M).
Flexibility and accessibility	Possibility to choose the time and place to follow the course (Arthur, A; Edna, E; Ivan, I; Marie, M)
	Access to training outside work hours (Carl, C; Fiona, F).
	Flexibility, 24/7 (Denise, D).
	Access to training that would be unavailable otherwise (Karen, K; Marie, M).
	Access to expertise that would be unavailable otherwise (Denise, D).
Modularity	Possibility of doing or re-doing only part of the course that is relevant to the employee (Edna, E).
Learning pace	Capacity to learn at your own speed since some people learn faster than others (Edna, E; Fiona, F; Ivan, I; Julien, J; Karen, K).
	Allows the firm to train more employees during the same period (Carl, C).
Learning style	Possibility of presenting the course material under various formats and of matching the different learning styles of employees (Ivan, I).
Interactive Feedback	Possibility of getting feedback by different means (telephone, fax, e-mail, camera, etc.) (Denise, D; Karen, K).
Privacy	Possibility of taking the course alone at home (Denise, D).
Customization	None
Evaluation	Possibility of evaluating employee progress during training (Edna, E).
Distribution of	The literature is always up-to-date; you don't have a folder that

Benefits	Explanation of the benefits
training material	collects dust on the shelves (Bert, B).
	Capability of acquiring knowledge that is rare or not often used, and to memorize it electronically for future use (Denise, D; Omer, O).
Consistent delivery	Assures that all employees receive the same training (Carl, C).
	The training is delivered in the same manner to all employees (Julien, J).
	Possibility of communicating information in an accurate and consistent manner (Denise, D).

Table 4: Perceived benefits of eLearning

Perceived benefits of eLearning	PME															
	Profile I strong				Profile II average				Profile III weak				Profile IV non-existent			
	C	D	K	L	B	E	M	O	A	F	I	J	G	H	N	P
Reduction of training costs (course, transportation, meals, lodging, time away from work)	x		x	x		x	x		x	x	x	x	x	x	x	x
Flexibility and accessibility	x	x	x	x		x	x		x	x	x	x	x	x	x	x
Modularity					x			x								
Learning pace (speed)	x		x	x		x				x	x	x	x			
Learning style	x	x	x	x	x							x				
Interactive feedback		x	x				x									
Privacy and independence		x										x				
Distribution of literature		x				x		x								
Evaluation	x	x	x	x		x										
Consistent delivery	x	x		x		x								x		
Customization																
Allow to remain competitive	x	x	x	x		x	x		x	x	x	x	x	x	x	x

The eLearning, and more specifically the benefits associated with it, seem to allow SMEs to offer more effectively training to their employees, and thus be more efficient. To this effect, according to OCDE

(2002), the investment of a company in the training and the update of the employees' skills is a key element of growth and sustainability, and SMEs need to exploit the eLearning to address their training needs in order to ensure their growth and their survival. Berris (2006) and Filipczak (1994) mention more or less the same thing, and for the latter, eLearning has to be part of the development of businesses in order to ensure their sustainability.

However, according to Industrie Canada (2001) and the Web-Based Education Commission (2000), if we want businesses to use eLearning, barriers in using eLearning need to be removed or at least reduced. A culture more favourable to eLearning, in addition to the benefits associated with it, encourages companies to use eLearning (Schweizer 2004; Roy 2010). Therefore, the approaches to incite SMEs to use eLearning must include both actions to develop a culture more conducive to eLearning and actions to remove or reduce barriers when it comes to using eLearning.

According to Middleton (2003), if companies want to position themselves so that they can compete on a global scale, they will need better skilled employees, and in order to achieve this, they will need to embark on a cultural change towards training. Moreover, the cultural change must be transmitted and be adopted by all stakeholders, i.e. by SMEs, the various players in economic development and society in general.

The development of a culture leaning towards learning and eLearning passes, among other things, by valuing learning, and by having a better understanding of the eLearning (Nonprofit World 2002; OCDE 2002; Tanquist 2001). The comment issued by Denise illustrates indeed the need to develop a culture of learning and of enhance learning. She says: «*We must develop a learning culture, in society in general, because without education or training businesses cannot survive.* » (D:985-999) For its part, the comment issued by Ivan illustrates the need to learn more about eLearning. He says: « *There must be information sessions. People should be made aware of what is eLearning. They should be presented a demo of what the eLearning can do* ». For its part, Jules says: «*It is important that SMEs see prac-*

Andrée Roy

tical examples of eLearning, things that are already used by another company if you want them to invest or move in that direction. The best way to educate a group is to present the success of customers or other SMEs and to recommend them to verify this with them. [...] It is also necessary to develop success stories. » (J: 1546-1551:1557-1565:1582)

We need champions of eLearning for the promotion and the awareness of eLearning in companies. This promotion and awareness can be done by internal champions of eLearning (Tanquist 2001) as well as by external champions (OCDE 2002, Manufacturiers et exportateurs du Québec 2003; TechnoCompétences 2002). However, champions must have credibility and knowledge of eLearning. The comment issued by Bert clearly illustrates the need for external champions of eLearning. He says: « *Developing courses in-house is expensive and it takes a lot of time. We need a champion to lead the case.* » (B:576:581-584) For its part, Edna illustrates the need for external champions of eLearning. She says: « *I think it should be someone, like economic development agencies, to tell SMEs about what is available.* » (E:613-615) Monique's comment also illustrates the need for external champions. She says: « *The information spreads quickly around here. If a person is satisfied with the eLearning, it won't take long for everyone to know. You can use agencies or groups to circulate the information. [...] I think we should encourage suppliers to give seminars to show what they have as courses. They could provide examples of people or businesses that use their courses. [...] They could show the different possibilities of eLearning for various industries.* » M:423-427:848-851:861-866)

It is critical for an organization to determine what the overall learning strategy of the company is. The SME has to determine exactly what it is trying to accomplish with eLearning (Lustig 2002). Learning strategies need to be well thought-out, carefully implemented, and most importantly, they must satisfy the wider business needs and goals. The importance of getting learning strategies right is at the core of eLearning approval by SMEs and by employees (Berris 2006). The firm must see eLearning as a tool rather than a panacea (Lustig 2002). Karen illustrates indeed the need for a learning strategy. She says: « *The general manager decided to include training needs in the annual business planning and in the development plan of the company. Upper management sees the importance of training and ongoing training. [...] We made the analysis according to the objectives. [...] We have online courses, as our courses on forklift and health and safety, all our production employees have to follow and redo them occasionally in order to get certified or re-certified. [...]They go online and do the courses. [...] We also have practical evaluations* » (K:103-108:117-119: 378-387: 610-614).

As previously mentioned, in addition to actions leading to the development of a culture more conducive to eLearning, actions should be undertaken to remove or to reduce barriers in using eLearning if we want to encourage SMEs to use eLearning. To this end, various actions including the upgrading of employees' skills in technology and the eLearning, offering technical support, the development of a toolbox, and the increase in bandwidth in some regions must be undertaken.

Among the factors that discourage SMEs and employees from using the eLearning, we find the lack of knowledge towards this one and of the technology (Zielinski 2000). Hector's comment is an example, he says: « *First, it is necessary that SMEs are equipped with people who can prepare the material for the eLearning. The IT equipment and the applications have to work. [...]. People who do the promotion have to know what they are talking about. It will take trained people to promote eLearning to other businesses.* » (H:386-398:410-412) Thus, in order to ensure that learners do not drop out or refuse to use eLearning, we must ensure that employees have the equipment, the software, the skills and the necessary knowledge needed to use the eLearning (Tanquist 2001; Zielinski 2000). Ivan gives us an example of the necessity to train employees, he says: « *Employees do not have all the necessary knowledge. We might have to train them before they can use computers and eLearning.* » (I:822-830) It is also necessary to provide basic courses for those who do not know how to use computers. Jules's comment goes in this direction, he says: « *Some of our employees do not have the knowledge and skills necessary [...].* » (J:654-658)

One of the factors which also discourage businesses to use eLearning is the lack of support available. Thus, in order to ensure that SMEs and learners do not drop out or refuse to use the eLearning, they must be given the necessary support to use the eLearning (Industrie Canada 2001; Roffe 2004; Web-Based Education Commission 2000; Zielinski 2000). To this effect Ivan said: « *It will take some support. There are some people who do not know how to download and install the necessary software.* » (I: 886-901) He adds: « *Universities or another organization should make resources available by e-mail or telephone, to provide a consulting service for SMEs. They could also leave a phone number that people could call, say between 4:00 pm and 6:00 pm, if they have questions. The questions would be answered by students, this would be part of their training and this would be an improvement for the business community. This would be a way to get people interested.* » (I:1086-1098) For its part, Denise says : « *It is necessary to speak the language of SMEs and employees.* » (D:1020)

Although, according to Harris (2005) and Roffe (2004), there are currently a large number of courses on the Internet and, even for SMEs, the lack of information about what is available on the Internet is one of the barriers identified in the use of eLearning; barriers identified by both authors and SMEs themselves. To overcome this barrier, some researchers (Harris 2005; Pantaziz 2002) suggested using tools to explore the availability of eLearning, and thus better understand what is available on the Internet. For its part, Tanquist (2001) suggests to create and distribute tools to help companies use eLearning. Gérôme's comment illustrates well this need of a toolbox. He says: « *The most interesting way would be to bring me a catalogue and to tell me what is available as training [...].* » (Gérôme G:595-597) Edna also expresses the need for a toolbox for SMEs or for access to different resources. She says: « *I think if the economic development agencies have libraries of courses pertinent to SMEs to train their employees, SMEs would see eLearning as a very effective way to provide training. I think that it is necessary to develop inventories of existing courses or to give access to portals such as "Soft Skill" where there is a library that contains hundreds of useful courses to SMEs to train their employees.* » (Edna E: 615-625 :627-643)

Finally, initiatives should be undertaken in order to increase bandwidth in the regions because this barrier reduces the ability of companies and employees to download training courses in eLearning format depending on where they are. Ivan's comment goes in this direction. He says: « *The Internet is the Internet. There are places where it is not fast [...] We need more bandwidth.* » (I:886-898) Gérôme also mentions the need for more bandwidth, he says: « *the speed of the line has to be greater (bandwidth), we should have a better network.* » (G:268-270) For his part, Jules says: « Some employees may not have access to the Internet at home. » (J:1055-1064)

Even though communication is not as such a barrier to the use of eLearning, it seems that the communication between SMEs and economic development agencies is not what it should be. Indeed, SMEs are under the impression that the agencies do not know their needs and that the programs they offer are not fitted to their needs. These problems are not directly related to eLearning, but would have an impact on how SMEs can fulfill their needs. They could possibly be mitigated through various outreach initiatives emanating from the economic development agencies via an action plan.

5. Conclusion and discussion

An increasing number of SMEs in Atlantic Canada use eLearning to train their employees. They find the benefits associated with it are some of the key elements of their growth and their sustainability. The benefits that SMEs perceive from eLearning are similar to those listed in the literature review. These benefits are: a 24/7 availability, a great flexibility, the possibility to test acquired knowledge and to work with new or unknown material, an increased independence in the workplace, an increased privacy in learning, an adaptation to the individual's speed and needs, a reduction in the training time, a faster upgrade and distribution of the training material, an increased training speed, a reduction of the time lost from work due to training, a reduction of travel by plane, a reduction in the training costs (training, meals, hotel, travel), a consistent delivery of the course content compared to a teacher, and the possibility of personalizing learning. The other perceived benefits that could encourage SMEs to use eLearning are: a fast upgrade of the employees, a reduction of the stress and nervousness associated with training and with the quality of the courses available. The employees also see a specific benefit to eLearning which is the possibility of developing their knowledge and advancing their careers.

A number of pre-requisites could constitute the core of an action plan to further enable eLearning in SMEs. The first pre-requisite is the need to develop an eLearning culture within the organization where managers and employees are truly motivated and committed to using eLearning because they believe it is essential to their individual development and to their organisation's development. This implies greater awareness and promotion of eLearning's value through the dissemination of knowledge among SMEs as to the nature, possibilities and advantages of eLearning for workplace training, and as to the supply and appropriateness of eLearning services and products available. A second pre-requisite is the need to lower the present barriers to the efficient and effective use of eLearning by SMEs. This implies that employees possess the computer knowledge and skills required to use eLearning effectively, and that they be provided with computers and eLearning software that are user-friendly and appropriate to the task at hand. This also implies better management and technical support of employees with regard to eLearning, support which was found lacking in a number of SMEs. Champions must also be identified, inside and outside of SMEs, to promote eLearning. Last but not least, learning strategies have to be developed to satisfy business needs and goals.

Governments, economic development agencies, universities and society in general also have a role to play in this transition from traditional training to eLearning, which is to develop a culture more conducive to training and eLearning as well as to facilitate access to eLearning in order to ensure the growth and survival of SMEs.

References

APECA. (1998) État de la petite entreprise et de l'entrepreneurship dans la région de l'Atlantique 1998. APECA. Direction générale des politiques et des programmes.

APECA. (2005) État de la petite entreprise et de l'entrepreneurship dans la région de l'Atlantique 2005. Moncton: Direction générale des politiques et des programmes.

Baldwin-Evans, K. (2004) Employees and eLearning what do the end-users think? Industrial and Commercial Training, Vol. 36 No. 7, pp. 269-274.

Bassi, L.J. and Van Buren, M.E. (1999). The 1999 ASTD state of the industry report. *Training & Development*, Vol 53, No. 2, pp 3-27.

Berris, J. (2006) "A job like mine", *E.learning Age*, October 26, p 26.

Brady, A. (1995) Small is as small does. *Journal of Business Strategy*, Vol. 16, No. 2, pp. 44-52.

EIU. (2004) Europe company: Making the most of eLearning. Economist Intelligence Unit. EIU ViewsWire.

Filipczak, B. (1994) The training manager in the '90s. *Training, 31*(6), 31-35.

Halkett, R. (2002) ELearning and how to survive it. *Industrial and Commercial Training*, Vol. 34, No. 2, pp. 80-82.

Harris, P. (2005) Small businesses bask in training's spotlight. *T + D, 59*(2), 46-52.

Homan, G. and Macpherson, A. (2005) ELearning in corporate universities. *Journal of European Industrial Training*, Vol. 29 No. 1, 75-90.

Industrial and Commercial Training. (2001) Employees ready for eLearning revolution. *Industrial and Commercial Training*, Vol. 33, No. 2, pp. 4-5.

Industrie Canada (2001) *L'évolution de l'apprentissage en ligne dans les collèges et les universités*. Saisie le 19 mars 2002, de http://www.rescol.ca/mlg/sites/acol-ccael

Jayawarna, D., Macpherson, A. and Wilson, R. (2007), Training **commitment and performance in manufacturing SMEs; Incidence, intensity and approaches,** *Journal of Small Business and Enterprise Development*, 14 (2), 698-720.

Journal of European Industrial Training. (2002) ELearning "set to boom" in Europe. *Journal of European Industrial Training*, Vol. 26, No. 6/7, pp. 4.

Kenyon, H. S. (2002) Learning Online From the Front Line. *Signal*, Vol. 56, No. 6, pp. 49-51.

Lustig, D. (2002) "How to transition to eLearning", **Pharmaceutical Executive,** Vol. 22, No. 11, pp. 114-116.

Manufacturiers et exportateurs du Québec. (2003) La formation par les TIC ou eLearning: le pourquoi et le comment: guide d'aide à la décision en contexte manufacturier. Montréal: Manufacturiers et exportateurs du Québec.

Matlay, H. (1999) Vocational education and training in Britain: A small business perspective. *Education & Training*, Vol 41, No. 1, pp 6-13.

Melymuka, K. (2002) "Executive Education on a Shoestring", *Computerworld*, Vol. 36, No. 11, pp. 24-25.

Middleton, C. (2003) The rate of learning must be greater than the rate of change. *Industrial and Commercial Training, 35*(6/7), 306-308.

Miles, M.B. and Huberman, A.M. (1994) *Qualitative Data Analysis: An Expanded Sourcebook*, 2nd Edition, Thousand Oaks, California: Sage Publications.

Mittelstaedt, J.D., Harben, G.N. and Ward, W.A. (2003) "How small is too small? Firm size as a barrier to exporting from the United States", *Journal of Small Business Management,* Vol 41, No. 1, pp. 68-84.

Nonprofit World (2002) Reach Out and Train Someone: The Many faces of distance Learning. *Nonprofit World*, Vol. 20, No. 2, pp. 24-29.

OCDE. (2002) *La formation des dirigeants des PME*. Paris: Éditions de l'OCDE.

Pantaziz, C. (2002) "Maximizing ELearning to Train the 21st Century Workforce", *Public Personnel Management*, Vol. 31, No. 1, pp. 21-26.

Perez, S., and Foshay, R. (2002) "Adding Up the Distance: Can Developmental Studies Work in a Distance Learning Environment?", *T.H.E. Journal*, Vol. 29, No. 2, pp. 19-24.

Roffe, I. (2004) ELearning for SMEs: Competition and dimensions of perceived value. *Journal of European Industrial Training, 28*(5), 440-455.

Roffe, I. (2007) Competitive strategy and influences on eLearning in entrepreneur-led SMEs. *Journal of European Industrial Training,* Vol. 31 No. 6, 416-434.

Rosenberg, M. (2002) "ELearning Trends in the Pharma Industry", *Pharmaceutical Executive*, Vol. 22, No. 10, pp. 114-115.

Roy, A. (2010) SMEs: How to Make a Successful Transition From Conventional Training Towards eLearning. *International Journal of Advanced Corporate Learning, Vol. 3, No. 2,* pp.21-27.

Schweizer, H. (2004) ELearning in business. *Journal of Management Education, 28*(6), 674-692.

Sloman, M. (2001) ELearning Revolution: from Propositions to Actions. CIPD.

Tanquist, S. (2001) Marathon eLearning. T + D, 55(8), 22-24.

Taran, C. (2006) Enabling SMEs to deliver synchronous online training – practical guidelines. Campus-Wide Information Systems, 23(3), 182-195.

TechnoCompétences (2002) ELearning: guide pratique de l'apprentissage virtuel en enterprise. Montréal: TechnoCompétences.

Tyler, K. (2001) ELearning: Not just for e-normous companies anymore. *HRMagazine, 46*(5), 82-88

Web-Based Education Commission. (2000) *The Power of the Internet for Learning: Moving from promise to practice*. Washington, DC: Government Printing Office.

Willging, P.A. and Johnson, S.D. (2004) Factors that Influence students decision to drop out of online courses. *Journal of Asynchronous Learning Networks*, Vol 2, No. 4, pp. 105-118.

Wolff, J.A. and Pett, T.L. (2000) "Internationalization of small firms: An examination of export competitive patterns, firm size, and export performance", *Journal of Small Business Management*, Vol 38, No. 2, pp 34-47.

Yin, R.K. (1994) *Case study research: Design and methods*, 2nd Edition, Thousand Oaks, California: Sage Publications.

Young, K. (2002) "Is eLearning delivering ROI?", *Industrial and Commercial Training*, Vol. 34, No. 2, pp. 54-61.

Youngers, M. A. (2002) "ELearning goes interactive", *Pharmaceutical Executive*, Vol. 22, No. 5, pp. 146-152.

Zahner, J. (2002) "Teachers explore knowledge management and eLearning as models for professional development", *TechTrends*, Vol. 46, No. 4, pp. 11-16.

Zielinski, D. (2000) Can you keep learners online? *Training, 37*(3), 64-75

Sharing and Shaping Effective Institutional Practice in TEL Through the 3E Framework

Keith Smyth
Edinburgh Napier University, Edinburgh, UK

Editorial Commentary
At the level of Higher Education institutions, the case for introducing learning technologies and for developing innovative ways of learning and teaching with their help is generally made. However it can be a far cry between the purchase of software or hardware at institutional level, and the setting of strategies to develop technology-enhanced learning, and actual change at course and module level. Edinburgh Napier University in the UK has pioneered an institutional benchmark for such practice through its 3E (Enhance, Extend, Empower) framework, the implementation of which is discussed in this case study. Driven by student expectations of consistent blending of face-to-face and online support and interaction, the 3E Framework aimed at engaging academic staff in developing their own pedagogic practice to enhance learning through the use of technology. Part of the project was the embedding of the framework, built on socio-constructivist principles, into the MSc Blended and Online Learning course offered by the university to staff and with the move to a new Virtual Learning Environment faced by all staff. As a case study of institutional adoption of technology enhanced learning, this has much to offer Higher Education Institutions, and in keeping with the principles underpinning the project, the framework itself is an Open Educational Resource under a Creative Commons Licence.

Case Studies in eLearning

Abstract: This paper presents a case study covering the design, development, and implementation of an institutional benchmark for technology-enhanced learning which places an emphasis on the active use of technology to support key aspects of the learning, teaching and assessment experience. With a focus on issues including sharing good practice, collective ownership of TEL strategy and implementation, and role modelling discipline-specific possibilities, this paper describes the 3E (Enhance-Extend-Empower) Framework, how it is being implemented at Edinburgh Napier University, and how it is being used across the wider sector. The paper concludes with a consideration of next steps including evaluating internal engagement with, and external adoption of, the 3E Framework.

Keywords: 3E Framework, benchmarking, cascading, staff development, institutional strategy

1. Introduction

As Higher Education institutions seek to further embed technology-enhanced learning (TEL) within their course provision, and for addressing wider educational needs, we inevitably become more aware of the challenges to be faced in modelling what's possible for those who have yet to engage in technology-enhanced practice, valuing and sharing current good practice in a useful way, and establishing a common understanding about the place TEL has within our institutions.

In respect to the latter issue it has been common practice in many universities to introduce an 'institutional benchmark' for TEL, often based on a set of minimum expectations for what information and resources will be provided on the Virtual Learning Environment (VLE). While not without value, engagement with this kind of approach can be problematic if it is seen as a top down edict, as insensitive to different disciplines, or promoting a generic template for TEL based only on institutional technologies (Czerniewicz and Brown, 2009; Hardaker and Singh, 2011). In seeing these limitations in the 'minimum presence' guidance for the VLE previously provided to staff, and to take forward good practice in a jointly owned way, Edinburgh Napier University recently developed a new institutional benchmark for the use of technology in learning, teaching and assessment (Smyth et al, 2011).

Comprising a 3E Framework that is based on an Enhance-Extend-Empower continuum, the new benchmark advocates a 'small blends' approach as the starting point for making active use of technology to enhance key aspects of the learning and teaching experience, and provides guidance on how technology can be used to support activities that extend the learners choice and control over how they learn, and to empower them to learn in ways that reflect as closely as possible the professional environments they are preparing for. To model general and discipline-specific good practice the 3E Framework provides illustrative examples for a range of learning and teaching activities, and examples of modules in different subject areas mapped to the framework. The 3E Framework has also been designed as platform independent, and to model uses of institutional and external technologies in ways that are easy for educators to grasp and see the potential of.

This paper explores the design of the 3E Framework and its successful application in staff development contexts, how it is being used to inform thinking about TEL in alignment with important strategic initiatives including the move to a new VLE, and the ways in which staff at Edinburgh Napier are being given ownership of the 3E Framework through its embedding in learning and teaching awards, establishing of local champions, and the authoring of good practice exemplars.

With a strong focus on respecting practitioners, effective modelling of practice, and the sharing of lessons learned, this paper will conclude with an overview of how other institutions have been adapting and working with the 3E Framework to support their own staff in TEL initiatives since its publication under Creative Commons as an open educational resource in late 2011.

2. TEL at Edinburgh Napier

As is the case within most tertiary education institutions, the use of technology to enhance learning, teaching and assessment is viewed as a core aspect of the student and staff experience at Edinburgh Napier University. A commitment to TEL has long been reflected within institutional strategy, major initiatives including the cross-institutional TESEP (Transforming and Enhancing the Student Experience through Pedagogy) project (Comrie et al, 2009), and also in the provision of institutional technical guidance in using institutionally-owned and external technologies in learning and teaching.

While predominately used in undergraduate provision, TEL is increasingly commonplace in supporting postgraduate programmes and in widening the University's reach into the areas of continuing professional development (CPD) and work-based learning. TEL has also become a key mechanism for meeting student's wider academic and support needs, particularly around induction activities for new students and articulation activities for direct entrants joining from FE.

However, while relatively widespread TEL is by no means fully embedded across the University. Feedback from a major institutional evaluation in 2009 highlighted this as a concern amongst our students, who expressed a strong expectation for all their modules to offer a balance of face-to-face and online support and interaction. This also underlined for the institution the discrepancy on the one hand between student expectations and the good TEL provision offered in some modules, and on the other the arguably outdated expectations around how the institutional VLE should be used that were encapsulated within the institutional benchmark still in place at the time of the evaluation.

At the time of adopting WebCT as the institutional VLE in 2004, the institutional vision recognised the opportunities offered by digital, predominantly online technologies to underpin 'traditional' campus based teaching, and to improve distance learning provision. As was commonplace in many institutions, and in some still is, our strategy for adopting TEL included a set of 'minimum presence' requirements for modules on the VLE which comprised centrally located information (timetable and module descriptor) and information provided by the module leader (to include as a minimum a statement on how the VLE was to be used for the module in question).

This aimed to provide an equitable student experience, but also to set a level of expectation of staff that was not too onerous. Indeed while staff were encouraged to go beyond the 'minimum presence' in their use of the VLE, the minimum presence itself could be easily established by programme administrators with little input from module leaders. Consequently, while many academics did move beyond the 'minimum presence' in their use of the VLE and other technologies, many did not and data available in 2009 suggested around a quarter of academic staff had yet to log-in to the VLE. From the staff survey and interview strand of the institutional evaluation undertaken, it became apparent that some staff did not view institutional expectations of how to use VLE as aligning well with how they wanted or needed to teach within their own discipline area, and felt that the VLE was quite constraining as a teaching space in comparison with other technologies

Views of this kind, particularly around institutional expectations versus the individual and contextual needs of academic staff, are not uncommon or to be unexpected. Many researchers have noted the tension that exists between institutional strategy and departmental or individual pedagogic practice in the use of technology in learning and teaching, and have underlined the need to strike a balance between both whereby a clear institutional direction also leaves space for autonomy and creativity (Stiles and York, 2007; Nichols, 2008; Czerniewicz and Brown, 2009; Freesen, 2010). This is not an easy balance to strike and requires a recognition, as Jackson (2011) observes, of institutional culture being pluralistic, contested and in a continual state of being formed and reformed through social relations. In Jackson's (*ibid*) recent evaluation of VLE adoption, it was the tension between the overwhelming power exerted by senior management and the individualistic nature of staff (including the enthusiastic, neutral and un-enthusiastic) that 'gridlocked' the institution and limited VLE uptake.

In the time that has elapsed since the initial adoption of WebCT as the institutional VLE at Edinburgh Napier, many of the academic staff who are engaging in technology-enhanced practice have become more confident in using technology and TEL has become more embedded within academic practice generally. This has seen a steep increase in the use of non-institutional technologies (including social networking platforms and read/write web tools) in learning, teaching and assessment. However pockets of no or minimum use remain, and as a means to meet student expectations, address dated expectations around VLE usage, and to move TEL forward across the institution (both for those yet to engage and for those who have good practice to build upon), in early 2011 the development of a new institutional 'Benchmark for the Use of Technology in Modules' was approved by the University.

3. Development of the 3E Framework

Rather than establishing a standard 'minimum presence' on the VLE as the starting point for TEL practice, the new Benchmark for the Use of Technology in Modules advocates "the active use of technology to meaningfully enhance the learning, teaching and assessment experience" (Smyth et al, 2011). This is encapsulated within the ethos of the 3E Framework that is the focus of the new benchmark, and which comprises an Enhance-Extend-Empower continuum (as shown in Figure 1).

Enhance	Extend	Empower
Adopting technology in simple and effective ways to actively support students and increase their activity and self-responsibility	Further use of technology that facilitates key aspects of students' individual and collaborative learning and assessment through increasing their choice and control	Developed use of technology that requires higher order individual and collaborative learning that reflects how knowledge is created and used in the professional environment

Figure 1: The 3E Framework enhance-extend-empower continuum

The 3E Framework is designed to help inform good practice in technology-enhanced learning, teaching and assessment, with an emphasis on considering what is appropriate to the context (i.e. subject, level, TEL experience of the tutor) in question. As a continuum it essentially illustrates how technology can be harnessed to: increase active learning (Enhance); give students direct responsibility for key aspects of their learning (Extend); and underpin more sophisticated activities that reflect the nature of learning and working in professional environments (Empower).

As presented within the institutional benchmark itself, which is available both as a document and as an online interactive resource (http://bit.ly/sUHeWk), the 3E Framework includes illustrative examples of TEL for a range of learning, teaching and assessment activities, and also a series of examples of University modules from across disciplines that are 'mapped' to the framework. This twin approach to illustrating good practice is to provide general guidance on using technology to address particular learning and teaching needs or challenges (e.g. teaching large cohorts, supporting group work), and to provide discipline-specific examples of effective TEL practice by School and Faculty members.

The 3E Framework, and associated guidance, was originally developed and refined within the context of the aforementioned cross-institutional TESEP project (Comrie et al, 2009) as a means of helping practitioners redesign their courses to increase learner autonomy, choice and engagement through blending classroom and online opportunities. The 3E Framework is based primarily on socio-constructivist principles, and as the continuum and different examples (Figures 2 and 3) will hopefully suggest it places a strong emphasis on students actively taking a lead in their learning through: creating or co-creating relevant resources for themselves and others; undertaking investigative and problem-based tasks; and engaging with others in their discipline area and wider professional communities. Engagement throughout the learning process is a central theme, as is the development of the broader skills and knowledge increasingly required within and beyond formal education.

While the 3E Framework sets out to model a continuum of TEL practice from the simple-but-effective through to more sophisticated, higher order forms of learning, there are a number of important points we are striving to make clear to our academics in their engagement with the 3E Framework:

- Although the 3E levels represent a continuum, they should not be viewed as mutually exclusive. In any single module, there may be a range of learning tasks and activities that align with any of the levels in the framework albeit new un-

dergraduates may be most appropriately engaged in Enhance activities
- While the 3E Framework is most likely to be applied within a modular context, it can equally be applied to designing and support progression across a programme of study
- The 3E Framework does not promote the Empower level as an ideal. Tutors and their students will start from (and end up at) different points on the 3E continuum in terms of using TEL in a particular learning, teaching and assessment context.
- As students transition along the 3E continuum, the tutor is relinquishing more control and responsibility. While this brings benefits, it can take adjusting to and requires the tutor to be comfortable with assuming facilitating or, in some contexts, even co-learning roles.

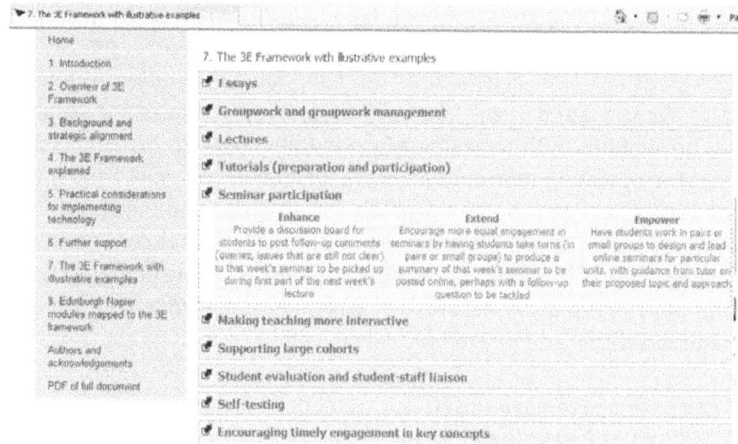

Figure 2: Illustrative 3E Framework examples relating to seminar participation

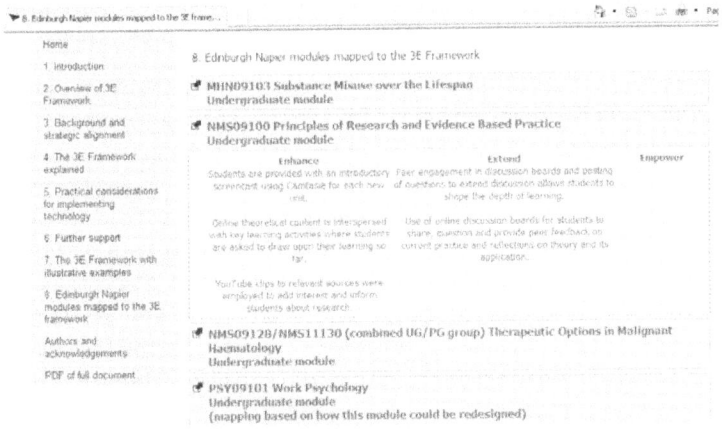

Figure 3: Example 3E Framework mapping to an existing undergraduate module

4. Implementation and embedding

Edinburgh Napier introduced the 3E Framework in November 2011, so at the time of writing the institution is approaching a year within which various implementation and embedding activities have been undertaken around the 3E Framework as the new institutional benchmark for TEL. While engagement amongst staff has been very encouraging thus far, we are mindful of previous experience around the former VLE benchmark, and the need to take a more multifaceted approach if we are to reach staff who are yet to engage with technology as well as those who are new to the 3E Framework itself. We have sought to do this by combining alignment with current institutional initiatives with other activities intended to help extend the reach of the 3E Framework, and with a deliberate focus on striking the balance between strategy and ownership discussed earlier by adopting a blend of 'bottom-up', 'middle-out' and 'top-down' activities - an approach which has proven effective for engagement with TEL strategy in other institutional contexts (Walker et al, 2011).

4.1. Embedding within professional development provision

While new to the institution the 3E Framework (in earlier form as the 3E Approach) is already implemented within Edinburgh Napier's MSc Blended and Online Education, where it provides the curriculum design model for the programme. The MSc BOE is an online programme for academics and other education professionals, and aims to engage participants from the outset in developing their skill and expertise as online educators while modelling good practice along the way. This is achieved through the embedding of the 3E Framework within the programme, particularly in relation to the first three modules which are designed to each of the Enhance, Extend and Empower stages (Figure 4).

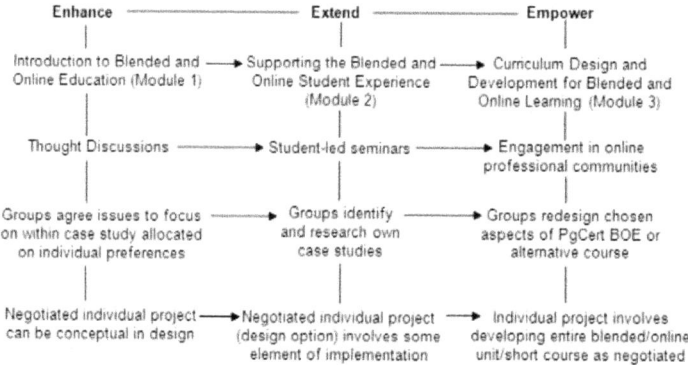

Figure 4: How the 3E Framework underpins the core modules of the MSc BOE

In implementing the 3E Framework across the three core modules of the MSc BOE, the intention is build upon the well-established concept of scaffolding to move participants to a position of expertise in a structured but relatively rapid way, and to ensure that by the end of Module 3 Pg Cert completers and continuing participants will be equipped to sustain their own professional development. As Figure 4 indicates, this involves a move from tutor-led seminars in Module 1 to participant-led seminars in Module 2 that provide an opportunity to research a topic, and to develop skills in preparing and facilitating online discussions that can be taken back into the participants own teaching practice. Similarly, in relation to individual work, in Module 1 participants undertake a project in designing for TEL that can be conceptual, but by Module 3 move on to producing a blended or online course that is ready to 'go live'. The 3E Framework-underpinned approach on the MSc BOE has proved successful to date, with an effective impact on the knowledge, skills and professional teaching practice of programme participants that is described more fully elsewhere (Smyth, 2009). What is important to the embedding of the 3E Framework across the institution is that Edinburgh Napier academics who take the programme gain an in-depth experience and insight into the nature of the framework, and how activities informed by it can be implemented in practice. They also study the 3E Framework when exploring curriculum design models for blended and online courses in Module 3 of the programme.

The institution is also focused on embedding the 3E Framework within Continuing Professional Development (CPD) provision, and from session 2011/12 all TEL-related seminars, workshops and short courses in the Professional Development Programme will explore applications of the 3E Framework to participants' own practice. Tailored support for module teams and subject groups is now beginning to be provided in their adoption of the 3E Framework, while the theme for the recent annual staff conference was 'Enhancing, extending and empowering student learning within online environments' and provided a range of opportunities for engagement with the 3E Framework

4.2. Alignment with move to new institutional VLE

In implementing the 3E Framework across the institution, we have drawn from the experience of previous educational transformation initiatives (Comrie et al, 2009; Mayes et al, 2009) and sought to align the introduction of the 3E Framework with other major strategic initiatives – specifically, the current move to Moodle as our new institutional VLE. A major programme of activities has been in place over the academic year 2011/12 to support staff in making the transition to Moodle which will go live across the institution from September

20212. This has required all staff to revisit their use of technology to a greater or lesser extent, and central to this process are new Faculty Learning Technologists who are providing academics with the support they need to adjust their resources and activities to the new environment, and to raise awareness of the 3E Framework. This face-to-face support has been complemented by the short online staff development course 'Meet Moodle', which over 250 staff have completed and which includes a collaborative activity 'Technology easy as 1-2-3E' as means of exploring and applying the 3E Framework and generating further examples to share.

4.3. Ownership and dissemination

The institution has sought to place ownership of the 3E Framework with academic staff on a number of levels. The 3E Framework and associated guidance was developed iteratively, with the University's Learning, Teaching and Assessment Committee overseeing and signing off the development of the framework and a wider pool of colleagues from across the University reviewing and commenting on work on progress throughout. Many of these colleagues mapped their own TEL practice from one or more of their own modules to the 3E Framework to ensure it went live with a rich range of discipline-specific examples from across the Schools and Faculties for staff to engage with and learn from.

The University LTA Strategy is underpinned by a widely used interactive LTA Resource Bank (bit.ly/OPKn6A) that contains a wide range of LTA case studies which include a reflective analysis of the impact of the approach taken. Staff can contribute case studies to the Resource Bank at any time, and the submission of case studies is also the means by which staff put forward their work for annual Learning, Teaching and Assessment awards. Each case study is tagged to enable staff to easily locate relevant case studies based on criteria including LTA approach, subject, and year of study. Any case study which was TEL-related was tagged with one or more of the 3E levels prior to the 3E Framework going live. This allowed the 3E Framework to be applied retrospectively in recognising existing good practice, and is an important message to underline in relation to a key purpose of the 3E Framework which is to capture and disseminate current good practice while informing future practice. The tagging of existing and new case studies in the Resource Bank to the relevant 3E levels provides staff with another means to locate real example applications of the Framework (Figure 5).

In addition to the aforementioned, a new Teaching Fellows Special Interest Group in Technology-Enhanced Learning (SIG-TEL) has been formed. This autonomous network comprises Senior Teaching Fellows, Teaching Fellows and other academic staff from across the Faculties, and has come together to help promote and disseminate good practice. The SIG-TEL has decided to focus their cross-Faculty activities for their first year of running on supporting the adoption of the 3E Framework and the move to Moodle, to provide further local support and ownership of developments.

Perhaps ultimately though, staff ownership of the 3E Framework lies within it being a descriptive rather than descriptive framework. It models possible ways of doing things from which the individual can adapt and implement as they see fit, with the only requirement being that they have at least two activities at the Enhance level (using institutional or other tools) within each of their modules.

4.4. Recognising and celebrating good practice

Beyond using the 3E Framework to retrospectively highlight good practice by mapping existing modules to the framework, and using it within staff development events to begin routinely gathering new applications of the 3Es, the recent annual learning and teaching conference (themed around the framework) featured LTA awards for best practice at the Enhance, Extend and Empower levels (bit.ly/HKlxnN). This brought forward a number of new case studies for the LTA Resource Bank, and in recognising best practice at each of the levels had two other important outcomes. The first was in bringing to the fore colleagues doing amongst the best TEL work within the institution, and by having separate awards for Enhance, Extend and Empower the second important outcome was in reinforc-

Case Studies in eLearning

ing the idea that each of the 3E levels are of equal value and validity in implementing TEL.

Figure 6: Case study in the University LTA Resource Bank

4.5. Establishing local champions

Establishing local champions that can provide contextualised local support to colleagues within schools and departments is widely accepted as critical to the successful implementation, uptake and sustainability of TEL initiatives, strategies and resources (Sharpe et al, 2007; Czerniewicz and Brown, 2009; Fresen, 2010; Walker et al, 2011). Internally there are a number of staff from across the Faculties on sponsored places to study the Pg Cert element of the MSc BOE programme, which carries a SEDA professional award in Embedding Learning Technologies. This is part of an institutional-wide initiative to establish accredited 'online educators' in every School, and many of these staff will act as 'local champions' for the 3E Framework through sharing discipline-related TEL examples using the framework, assisting in one-to-one and group staff development sessions, and writing up emerging good practice informed by the framework as cases for the LTA Resource Bank.

5. Staff engagement and uptake

Overall staff engagement with the 3E Framework, and their acceptance of the framework as the new institutional Benchmark for the Use of Technology in Modules, has been very positive to date. Beyond the number of staff who have thus far contributed module mappings for potential inclusion in the 3E Framework itself (in excess of 80), or who have contributed case studies for the LTA Resource Bank (around 30), we have been encouraged by the staff who submitted proposals to run 'Learning from Experience' sessions around the 3E Framework at the recent staff conference. We have also seen engagement with the 3E Framework emerge in other important ways including:

- Coursework submitted by staff on the Pg Cert Learning and Teaching in Higher Education, and staff workshops within Schools, discussing local embedding of the 3E Framework
- Applications from prospective Teaching Fellows coming forward that discuss the applicant's engagement with the 3E Framework and proposing how they will help embed the Framework
- Presentations and agenda items for School and Faculty LTA meetings

6. Adoption of 3E Framework within the sector

Partly because the 3E Framework is derived from a cross-institutional project with a commitment to sharing outputs, although mainly due to a sense that other institutions may be seeking a move away from 'conventional' TEL benchmarks, the 3E Framework was published under a Creative Commons license to allow for potential re-use and adaptation. The wider relevance and applicability of the framework may be borne out by the number of institutions who have expressed an interest in adapting it, or who are already actively doing so. Current developments include:

- The forthcoming introduction of a new institutional TEL Quality Framework at York St John's University that is underpinned by the 3E Framework (bit.ly/UBQnnF)
- The recent launch at Plymouth Marjon University College of their adapted version of the 3E Framework including video introduction to the key concepts for their staff (bit.ly/MKtGsa)
- Application of the 3E Framework as an evaluation tool to gauge levels of VLE use across the institution at the University of York (bit.ly/RHmCO6)
-

This is an illustrative selection of 3E Framework applications that are at a well developed stage, and we are also aware of work-in-progress within other institutions to use the 3E Framework to inform online Masters programme developments, support various staff development initiatives, and to guide curriculum redesign as part of a government-funded education project in Greek schools. Furthermore, the 3E Framework has been put forward as a model for the HE sector to consider in a recent position paper commissioned for the Quality Assurance Agency's current Enhancement Theme of 'Developing and Supporting the Curriculum' (Fotheringham et al, 2012).

7. Conclusions

In seeking to move away from an institutional benchmark for TEL practice that was predominantly focused on the minimum information to be provided on the institutional VLE, and towards a benchmark that more accurately reflected the potential for using a range of technologies to effectively support learning, teaching, and assessment, our experience of introducing the 3E Framework at Edinburgh Napier has been encouraging. Staff have engaged well with initiatives related to introducing and embedding the framework across the institution, and while we are yet to formally evaluate engagement with the 3E Framework (which will be done in tandem with evaluating engagement with the new VLE in the next academic year) evidence is forthcoming in the range of ways discussed in this paper of an active initial wave of engagement and acceptance.

We have a number of mechanisms in place to ensure continued engagement, and are also encouraged by the uptake of the 3E Framework to support strategic and staff development initiatives within other institutions. We will shortly be undertaking an evaluation of the ways in which the 3E Framework has been used for different purposes within these institutions, and will use our findings to offer further guidance and resources on using the framework to the sector via Creative Commons.

Important pedagogical issues relating to implementing the 3E Framework need further exploration, including the role of the tutor at the 'Empower' level. Here the well-established distinction between the role of the tutor as sage versus guide-on-the-side arguably falls short, as do more recent notions of the tutor as a 'ghost in the wings' (Mazzolini and Maddison, 2006), as at the Empower stage the tutor will often be assuming at least a co-learning role and in some instances a 'less expert' learner role. We will seek to understand how staff respond to this, and to other implications of implementing the 3E Framework, in further qualitative research involving those who have adopted the framework.

8. Acknowledgements

The author, and colleagues who have helped develop the institutional guidance and staff provision around the 3E Framework, would like to acknowledge the contribution of Edinburgh Napier staff including the LTA Committee to supporting the development and implementation of the framework.

References

Comrie, A., Smyth, K. and Mayes, T. (2009) "Learners in control: the TESEP approach", In T. Mayes, D. Morrison, H. Mellar, P. Bullen and M. Oliver (Eds.), *Transforming higher education through technology-enhanced learning*, York, Higher Education Academy, pp. 208-234.

Czerniewicz, L. and Brown, C. (2009) "Intermediaries and infrastructure as agents: the mediation of e-learning policy and use by institutional culture", ", In T. Mayes, D. Morrison, H. Mellar, P. Bullen and M. Oliver (Eds.), *Transforming higher education through technology-enhanced learning*, York, Higher Education Academy, pp. 107-121.

Fotheringham, J., Strickland, K., and Aitchison, K. (2012) "Curriculum: directions, decisions and debate", The Quality Assurance Agency for Higher Education, [online], Last retrieved June 1st, 2012 from http://www.enhancementthemes.ac.uk/enhancement-themes/developing-and-supporting-the-curriculum.

Fresen, J.W. (2010) "Factors influencing lecturer uptake of e-learning", *LAMS and Learning Design*, Vol. 11, No. 1, pp. 81-97.

Hardaker, G. and Singh, G. (2011) "The adoption and diffusion of eLearning in UK universities: a comparative case study using Gidden's Theory of Structuration", *Campus Wide Information Systems*, Vol. 28, No. 4, pp.221-233.

Jackson, S. (2011) "Organizational culture and information systems adoption: a three-perspective approach", *Information and Organization*, Vol. 21, No. 2, pp. 57-83.

Mazzolini, M. and Maddison, S. (2006) "The role of the instructor as a guide on the side". In J. O'Donoghue (Ed.), *Technology-Supported Learning and Teaching: a Staff Perspective*, London, Information Science Publishing, pp 224-241.

Mayes, T., Morrison, D., Mellar, H., Bullen, P. and Oliver, M. (Eds.) (2009) *Transforming higher education through technology-enhanced learning*, York, Higher Education Academy

Nichols, M. (2008) "Institutional perspectives: the challenges of e-learning diffusion", *British Journal of Educational Technology*, Vol. 39, No. 4, pp. 598-609.

Sharpe, R., Benfield, G. and Francis, R. (2006) "Implementing a university e-learning strategy: levers for change within academic schools", ALT-J, Vol. 14, No. 2, pp. 135-151.

Smyth, K., Bruce, S., Fotheringham, J. and Mainka, C. (2011) *Benchmark for the use of technology in modules*. Edinburgh Napier University, [online], Last retrieved June 1st, 2012 from http://staff.napier.ac.uk/services/academicdevelopment/TechBenchmark/Pages/home.aspx

Smyth, K. (2009) "Transformative online education for educators: cascading progressive practice in teaching, learning and technology", In D.Remenyi (Ed), *Proceedings from the 8th European conference on e-learning*, University of Bari, Italy, 29th-30th October. Academic Conferences International, pp. 549-557.

Stiles, M. and Yorke, J. (2007) "Technology-supported learning: tensions between innovation, control and organisational and professional cultures", *Journal of Organisation Transformation and Social Change*, Vol. 3, No. 3, pp.251-267.

Walker, D., Sloan, D., Boyle, L. and Walsh, L. (2011) "Informing TEL strategy through formal and informal channels: a case study", *Campus Wide Information Systems*, Vol. 28, No. 4, pp.289-293.

Challenges in Developing e-Submission Policy and Practice

Alice Bird
Liverpool John Moores University, Liverpool, UK

Editorial Commentary

E-submission is a topical challenge facing most Higher Education Institutions. While the technology is relatively straightforward, the difficulties lie in the detail, since a straight exchange from paper submission to e-submission is not without its dangers, both administrative and political. This case study explores the transition over three years within one UK University from the perspective of major stakeholders, including the student body. The paper clarifies the interconnectedness of many academic sub-systems with the submission system, not just the feedback and learning processes but also progression and enrolment systems and quality assurance systems. The reflective conclusions of this case study urge the need to take into account prevailing cultures and sub-cultures in the institution and relative power relationships between stakeholders when introducing such a major change to working practices.

Abstract: In the current economic climate, higher educational institutions are seeking strategies to enhance the student learning experience and, at the same time, reduce administrative costs. Electronic submission of coursework, e-submission, is frequently perceived as one approach that can help achieve both of these objectives. However, this view fails to acknowledge the diverse needs of the key stakeholders (institutional strategic management, academic staff and the student body) and the increased influence of the latter on institutional policy development. This shift in powerbase imposes additional challenges for those responsible for developing and implementing high stakes institutional change initiatives, such as e-submission policy and practice. This paper begins by reviewing the background to developing and implementing electronic submission policy and practice, in the context of institutional cultures and orientations to academic development.

Alice Bird

It acknowledges increased influence of the student voice and enhanced difficulty in developing policy and practice when mediating between three equally powerful stakeholders; strategic management, academia and the student body. It offers an insight into the dynamics of these triumvirate influences through a three-year e-submission case study at one higher educational institution. The paper charts the progress of the case through three phases (feasibility study, pilot study and early stage implementation), highlighting the influences of the key stakeholders on outcomes and attempts to gain consensus on policy and practice. The paper concludes by reflecting on the experiences and findings from the case study and making recommendations on how other institutions might approach developing similar e-submission policy and practice.

Keywords: e-submission policy, institutional change, institutional compliance, academic freedom, student voice

1. Introduction

In the current economic climate, higher educational institutions are seeking strategies to enhance the student learning experience and, at the same time, reduce administrative costs. Electronic submission of coursework, e-submission, is frequently perceived as one approach that can help achieve both of these objectives. The affordances of web-based technologies and content repositories lend themselves well to the administrative aspects of submission receipting, electronic feedback, online moderation and overall rapid turnaround. However, this technological view of the process fails to acknowledge the diverse needs of the key stakeholders; institutional management, academic staff and the student body. It also ignores the current shift in influence on institutional policy development, brought about by increased attention to the student voice.

Electronic submission of coursework represents a high stakes cultural change in the way student work is submitted, marked and feedback provided. The three key stakeholders have diverse, but not necessarily, mutually exclusive objectives. Higher educational management are mindful that administrative costs need to be curtailed and view the handling of paper-based items of coursework as a non-essential activity. Their preference is for institutional compliance on e-submission to reduce costs and offer a consistent student experience. The student body, empowered by National Student Survey findings, seeks more flexible approaches to assessment and more timely and informative feedback on assessment. Members of academic staff continue to advocate academic freedom in choosing how to teach and assess students, with concerns about radical change in practice and disempowerment. For successful development of institutional policy and practice, these three groups must come together and agree an appropriate way forward.

This paper begins by considering the background to changes in institutional powerbases before charting a three-year case study aimed at implementing e-submission at one higher educational institution. It concludes by reflecting on the experience and making recommendations for other institutions considering similar development of e-submission policy and practice.

2. Background

The context of the current paper has resonance with many UK higher educational institutions as they respond to and prepare for changes in funding and anticipated increase in accountability demanded by students. Institutions are seeking to reduce costs, particularly those not associated directly with research or teaching. In many institutions, administrative and support activities have been or are being reviewed under the banner of improving the student experience. This focus on cutting costs coincides with increased power of the student voice through the medium of the National Student Survey. In particular, the outcomes of the survey continue to suggest sector-wide issues in meeting student expectations on assessment and feedback on assessment. In recent years, the National Union of Students (NUS) has proactively sought to engage institutions in addressing these issues through a series of campaigns. For many institutions, this has resulted in a three-way split in the institutional powerbase; institutional strategic management, academia and the student body, often represented by the local Student Union. At this point, it should be acknowledged that overall power within this triumvirate will differ from one institution to another depending on the predominant institutional culture.

The topic of culture in higher education is one that has been widely researched and discussed. Trowler (2008) presents an exploration into approaches to understanding higher education cultures, including references to macro, micro and meso level approaches. At the macro (organisational level), Trowler cites Berquist's four cultures (1992); collegial, managerial, developmental and negotiating. Whilst at the micro (individual) level, culture is defined in terms of the institution and its distinctiveness, e.g. Tierney (1988). An alternative meso level approach acknowledges a multiple cultural configuration which encompasses more open, dynamic and interactive concepts e.g. Alvesson (2002, pp.186-187). In an earlier study, Land (2001) also makes reference to organisational cultures and maps a set of orientations to academic development against conceptions of change. These orientations, opportunistic/entrepreneurial, reflective practitioner, interpretive-hermeneutic, romantic (outreach), professional competence activist-modellers, political strategist (pragmatist), consultant researcher, disciplinary, managerial/HRM, are adopted by practitioners promoting change in academic practice according to the context that they find themselves in. Groups and individuals involved in promoting change in academic practice are generally aware of the predominant and sub-cultures that exist within a particular institution. However, the shifts in power, with the student voice in the ascendancy, mean that they may need to review and revisit their approaches to implementing change.

As with any work-based or social relationship, it is easier to mediate between two parties than three. With three stakeholder groups influencing policy and practice, the direction of change can be swayed with one party often feeling disempowered by the perception of the other parties operating in league. This paper offers an insight into the dynamics of triumvirate influences through a three-year case study to develop and implement electronic submission policy and practice at one higher educational institution. The predominant organisational culture of the institution is generally acknowledged as managerial, with strategic leadership responsible for driving through change, but with sub-culture influences often aligned to specific subject disciplines. However, student contribution to development of policy has become more influential through proactive engagement by the Student Union and a strategic 'you say, we do' approach to improving the student experience.

3. Case study

The recommendation to introduce electronic submission of coursework (e-submission) first evolved from an institutional review of student administrative processes. The recommendations from the review were translated into a student experience review implementation project aimed at restructuring student support services and activities across the institution. Part of the review included an observation of activities in three centralised centres, processing student submissions of paper-based coursework items. This revealed a negative impact on student experience; in particular, issues associated with processing submissions at peak submission deadlines. The outcome was a recommendation to develop institutional policy and practice for the electronic submission of coursework. This recommendation was approved and strategically driven from the top through an institutional development project. The progress of the project through three phases, feasibility study, pilot study and early-stage implementation, constitutes the core of this case study, with references to triumvirate influences on the direction and outcomes.

3.1. Feasibility study

The feasibility study was initiated in September 2008 and conducted according to institutional principles based on the Prince2 methodology. A Project Board was convened, with a School Director appointed as the Chair and membership representatives drawn from each Faculty, relevant Central Service Teams and the Student Union. Faculty representatives, who were nominated by School Directors, for their general interest in teaching, learning and assessment, were not necessarily advocates for e-submission. An initial challenge was defining the project brief and initiation document. There was no explicit articulation from senior management of the rationale for e-submission policy and practice, other than fulfilling the recommendation within the student experience review. However, the general consensus of the project board was that the scope of the feasibility study should not be limited to exploring administrative benefits but should also cover pedagogical benefits. In particular, it was considered essential to explore potential improvements in the timeliness and relevance of feedback to students on assessment, in the light of the sector-wide dissatisfaction expressed in the 2007 and 2008 National Student Surveys.

The project objectives included, as a starting point, outlining the activities associated with the overall coursework management process. Defining the process was vital to gaining a better understanding of the potential role for technological support, as a preliminary stage in specifying technical and functional requirements. The project also sought to assess the needs and perceptions of key stakeholders, in particular academic staff and students. A final objective was to estimate the resource implications in moving from paper-based to electronic submission. A project reporting deadline was set for March 2009, in order to make recommendations for implementation in the academic year 2009/10. Figure 1 provides the final version of the outline process map, agreed after frequent iterations.

Developing the process map presented a further challenge to the Project Board, in terms of gaining consensus on the various activities. The process involves much more than submission, feedback and recording of grades. For example, submission of coursework is used as an indicator of a student's continued participation on a course, an essential item of information in tracking local and international students. The process map also took account of the fact that implementing e-submission would not necessarily guarantee e-marking, with some staff electing to continue marking printed copies of submitted coursework items. Refining the start/end points and various routes through the process generated some debate, with representatives from some subject areas having more clearly defined conceptualisations than others. However, defining an outline of the process proved invaluable for highlighting the overall complexity and also in demonstrating that recommendations for submitting coursework electronically could not be made in isolation from other activities that preceded or succeeded it. It was also used as the basis for specifying the technical and functional requirements for the technology

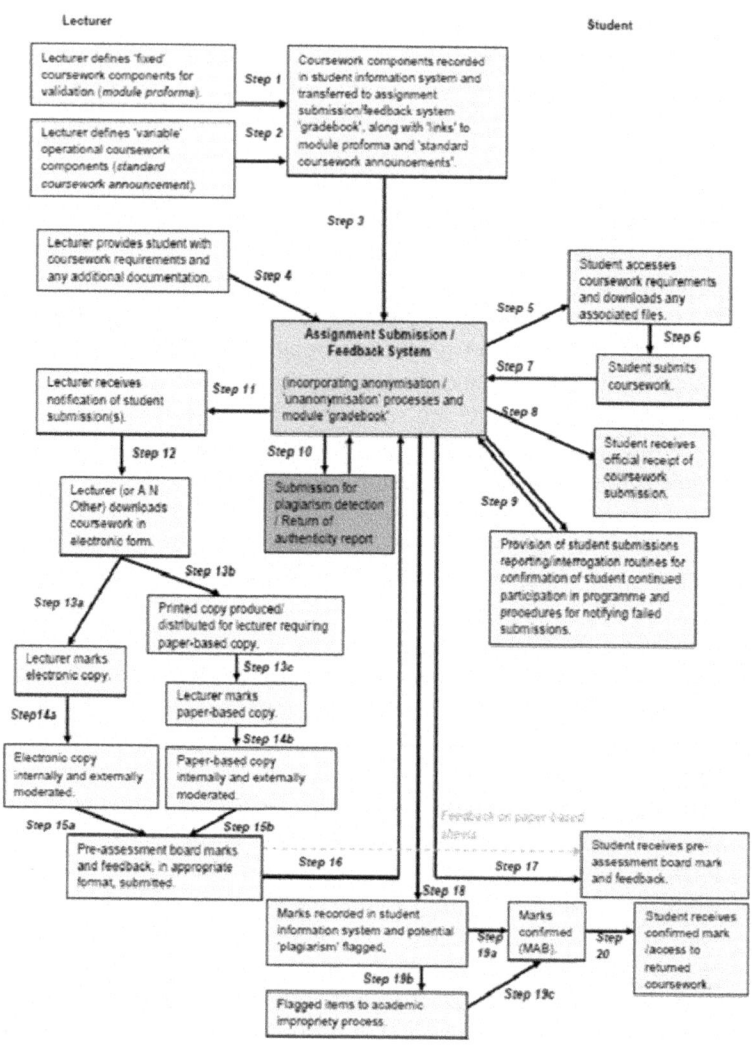

Figure 1: Outline process map

Faculty representatives consulted academic staff on types of assessment items classified as 'coursework' and implications for submission file types. This revealed considerable diversity in items, other than the standard text-based essay, report or portfolio. (See Table 1 below).

Table 1: Types of coursework item

Essays	Studio display
Class test (seen and unseen)	Video and audio recordings
Documentary exercises	Field notebooks
Research reports	Posters
Response papers	Data authenticity folders (confidential material)
Presentations (group and individual)	Dioramas
Performances	Log books/diaries
Portfolios	Drawings
Seminar journals	Computer programmes
Drawings	Mathematical items
Artistic rendering	Graphs
Physical models	Computer-generated models

The range of possible file types was equally diverse, although common text-based types were likely to predominate. (See Table 2 below)

Table 2: Example file types

MS Word	Web pages/HTML
MS Excel	CAD files
MS PowerPoint	Computer programmes
Pdf	ChemDraw
Video/audio	GIS
Image files	Other specialist software files

The possible file types indicated the need to identify a technological solution capable of supporting non-standard submissions. The assignment tool within the institutional virtual learning environment (VLE) was one solution that met this requirement. Users of an existing plagiarism detection service were keen to continue using it but the limited range of file types that it supported meant that it could not be the sole solution for electronic submission.

Student and academic staff consultations were also undertaken to assess perceived benefits and issues in implementing e-submission. Members of academic staff were also asked to comment on prior experience of e-submission. The Student Union co-ordinated the student consultation by inviting course representatives to carry out face-to-face interviews with students that they represented. Faculty consultation was undertaken through Project Board Faculty representatives sending out a set of standard questions by Faculty email lists. The total number of respondents was not recorded but a summary of the views of respondents from each of the six Faculties was collated into a general statement of perceptions and experiences.

The student consultation collated feedback from 30 course representatives who interviewed a total of 160 students. The majority of students interviewed (83%) suggested they would welcome electronic submission of coursework. Some perceived advantages included *'less travel for students who commute'* and, for international students, the ability to *'return home and still submit'*. However, there was some concern about the potential robustness and reliability of any system for supporting submission. In particular, students expressed concern about the ability of a system to handle high volumes of student submissions, at the same time. Other concerns related to potential failure to meet deadlines due to problems with their own internet connections or computer systems. When asked to comment on existing submission and feedback experiences, 76% thought deadlines were scheduled effectively, although some of the remainder felt that deadlines tended to be very close together. *'Quicker'* and *'more detailed'* feedback featured highly as a key area for improvement, with 32% receiving feedback over a month after submission and almost a quarter (23.4%) never receiving any feedback on assessment.

The Faculty consultation highlighted a wide variation of prior experience across the institution from individuals with in-depth experience of e-submission and e-marking to other members of staff having limited experience of technology, in general. The perceived benefits and issues reflected this diversity. In most cases, the benefits were considered only realisable with associated assumptions; in particular, a move to electronic marking and feedback. Tables 3 and 4 below summarise the perceived benefits and issues with associated assumptions.

Table 3: Faculty perceived benefits

Perceived Benefit	Assumption
Faster, more direct access by markers to submitted coursework	
'Greener' coursework submission approach	Overall reduced levels of printing
Reduced manual handling of paper-based coursework	Reduced levels of printing
More detailed and timely feedback	e-Marking and e-feedback
Easier deterrence/detection of collusion/plagiarism	Integration with plagiarism detection service

Table 4: Faculty perceived issues

Perceived Issues	Assumption
Failed submission due to students' own PCs/connections	Off-campus submission
Robustness and scalability of submission/feedback system	
Lack of staff/student ICT skills and confidence	
Lack of local staff support for changing practice	
Staff screen usage health and safety issues	e-Marking and e-feedback
Increased departmental printing cost	Staff opting to mark paper-based copies
Delays in receipt of coursework/provision of feedback	Staff opting to use Print Room service
Ability of technology to fulfil associated 'marking' requirements: anonymous, team, double and external	

The feasibility study concluded with the publication of a report and set of recommendations, incorporating a summary of associated resources and costs. The main recommendation was to implement a pilot study within Faculties in the academic year 2009/10 to assess the extent to which perceived benefits and issues were likely to be actual benefits and issues when scaling up to institution wide implementation. A second recommendation proposed further technological development and performance testing of submission via the VLE to ensure scalability to institutional requirements. The report also recommended expansion of central and local support to minimise institutional risk during the pilot phase. Finally, the report acknowledged the need to consider alternative approaches to assessment and not to simply replicate traditional modes of assessment within a technology enhanced learning environment. There was a strong belief that the affordances of technology could support alternative, more authentic methods of assessment that should be explored more widely.

The report was presented to the institutional strategic management group in May 2009. The recommendations to implement the pilot study and to undertake the technological work were approved. Additional resources for central and local Faculty-based support were not approved at this stage as a key objective was to reduce overall administrative and support costs.

Reflecting on the feasibility study, the division of power still seemed to be split mainly between strategic management and academic staff. Project Board meetings frequently returned to discussions on issues associated with academic staff engagement in e-submission. The project Chair played a vital role in keeping the project on track in achieving its objectives. The role of the student union was mainly consultative rather than a force for change. However, there were early indicators of the increasing influence of the local Student Union through lobbying in response to a National Union of Student (NUS) Higher Education Campaign. Working in collaboration with the institutional Learning Development Unit, *Mark My Words, Not My Name*, NUS (2008), was translated into a recommendation for institutional implementation of anonymous marking of coursework.

3.2. Pilot study

The second phase of the e-submission project was initiated in September 2009, following on from the recommendations of the feasibility study. The stepping down of the Chair from the Project Board resulted in a Faculty Dean being appointed to fulfil this role.

Preparation for the pilot study included the development of online support resources for staff and student participants prior to the start of the academic year. During August and September 2009, participating members of academic staff were recruited and identified specific module cohorts for the pilot. The pilot was implemented in 52 modules from a range of different programmes. A key aim was to ensure the pilot covered a diversity of subject disciplines, different cohort sizes and programme levels, different types of submissions (file types, sizes and single/multiple files) and range of student and staff levels of ICT competencies. In practice, although all Faculties participated in the pilot, engagement varied considerably with some Faculties involving whole subject areas, whilst others allowed self-nomination by individual members of staff. The latter tended to be techno-enthusiasts and this had to be taken into account when evaluating the pilot. Group and one-to-one hands-on training sessions were provided for participating staff in using the VLE assignment tool. In some cases, participating staff implemented e-submission for a single coursework assignment with one cohort, whilst others piloted e-submission with several cohorts in Semester 1 and Semester 2. Although the pilot required staff to use a specified submission tool, they were at liberty to determine how they marked coursework and provided feedback to students. Online help resources were provided for a range of methods for e-marking but instructions were also provided on how to batch submit coursework items for printing via the university print room.

Evaluation of the pilot study focused on three key areas; submission, marking and feedback. The methods used included online questionnaires issued to participating staff and students. Students were invited to participate in a post-submission questionnaire, whilst members of staff were invited to complete pre- and post-submission questionnaires in order to assess any shifts in their perceptions after engaging with e-submission. Triangulation of questionnaire findings was achieved through analysis of staff and student support calls throughout the pilot and more general feedback collated by the Faculty and Student Union representatives on the Project Board.

In parallel with the pilot study, technological development and performance testing was implemented. During the pilot, some additional requirements for augmentation of the VLE assignment tool emerged. In addition, the outcomes from a Higher Education Academy funded study at the University of Sheffield Hallam, Hepplestone et al (2010), focused on the use of a customisation of the tool that helped promote student engagement with feedback on assessment. A demonstration of the system to the Project Board and other members of academic staff resulted in a strong recommendation for acquisition of the customised version for any future phase of the project.

The participant response rate to online questionnaires was 49% of academic staff (25) and 17% of students (167). The outcomes of the evaluation suggested that only a few members of academic staff in the pilot had prior experience of e-submission. Most staff and student respondents rated their levels of ICT confidence as confident or very confident. However, approximately 5% of staff had limited or no confidence and expressed some apprehension in engaging in the pilot. Some staff and students had experienced technical issues during the pilot but both staff and students agreed that there were benefits for students, in particular, with the submission stage of the process. The main benefits included savings on travel time and costs and enhanced ability to submit at anytime and from any location. Some staff also acknowledged benefits through faster receipt of submissions, although some of those who chose to print out submitted coursework disagreed with this view. Members of staff were much more divided on the benefits when taking into account other stages in the process. Some were unhappy about feeling obliged to mark electronically, whilst others had issues in dealing with specific coursework types. Some members of staff also experienced difficulties in downloading very large files submitted by students or in dealing with multiple file submissions. The findings, in terms of whether students thought that submitting coursework electronically had enabled better and/or timelier feedback, were inconclusive. A slight majority (39%) thought it had but 30% did not and the remaining 31% were unsure.

When asked to rate their overall experience, two thirds of students considered the experience to be worthwhile or very worthwhile. A further 22% rated the experience as satisfactory whilst 11% believed the experience to be not worthwhile or (for two students) totally unsatisfactory. Despite the concerns raised by staff, 48% rated their overall experience as worthwhile or very worthwhile. A further 24% found the experience to be satisfactory but 28% considered their experience to be not worthwhile or totally unsatisfactory. In addition, staff continued to reiterate concerns about health and safety, issues with printing and overall capacity to cope with any scaling up of e-submission activity.

The findings from the evaluation demonstrated a need to accommodate the diversity in needs between staff and students. Many on both sides acknowledged benefits but the balance was swung in favour of students, in terms of convenience and savings to them. As a consequence, the Project Board developed a proposed 'third way' forward that would require, as a minimum expectation, e-submission for some but not all items of coursework. Hence, the main recommendation was for a phased implementation in 2010/11 based on the types of coursework item identified as most suitable, in the pilot study, for submitting electronically. This included items meeting the following criteria:

- A single file
- In Word or pdf format
- Of no more than 2000 words
- Submitted before the end of main assessment period

It was believed that assessments meeting these criteria would be more appropriate for academic staff to test out e-marking, to develop other steps in the submission/feedback process and to look at alternative approaches to delivering feedback electronically, e.g. voice feedback. This recommendation was approved by the strategic management group along with the agreement to implement the customisation of the native VLE assignment tool.

During the pilot study, the influence of the student voice on strategic engagement in institutional decision-making gained greater significance. A second NUS Higher Education Campaign, NUS (2009), focused on improvements to assessment and feedback and identified ten principles on which good feedback should be based. In addition, Government sponsorship for defining 'a reasonable student experience', through the National Student Forum, further raised the need for improved feedback on assessment along with some fundamental changes to teaching and learning organisation and practice in universities, NSF (2009). (The continued strategic contribution by students, at a national level, is evidenced in the report commissioned by HEFCE through the NUS on students' perspectives of technology in learning, teaching and assessment, as part of the Online Task Force consultation, HEFCE (2010)).

In the current case, the Student Union developed its own version of ten ways to make feedback better based on consultation with students. This was presented to the Academic Board, in May 2010, in the form of a printed document with real examples of positive and negative student experiences. The first three objectives were approved for implementation. These included a requirement for feedback deadlines to be published along with assessment, all feedback to be made available three weeks after the deadline and all feedback to relate to assessment criteria. Of these three objectives, the three week turnaround for feedback proved most contentious, with academic staff feeling that they had not been consulted in the decision-making process. As a sense of disempowerment emerged, academic staff became more aware of greater student influence and apparent collusion between strategic management and students in decision-making processes. This was further enhanced by other institutional changes to the academic framework and administrative processes which culminated in a feeling of initiative overload from the member of academic staff perspective.

3.3. Early stage implementation

During the academic year 2010/11, a number of factors combined to transform the proposed early stage implementation into an extended pilot rather than wide-spread implementation. Academic staff initiative overload referred to earlier was one factor and there was also a need to align more generally with other institutional policies, including the proposal for anonymous marking. Participation was wider than in the previous pilot study, with increased general awareness of a developing e-submission policy. This led to wider debate amongst the academic community, with the main union representing academic staff questioning aspects of policy and practice, already raised as perceived issues by staff.

Union concerns about health and safety resulted in a revision of the university's safety code of practice on visual display equipment to accommodate laptop and tablet devices. This did not lead to the identification of any specific e-submission and e-marking safety issue, although staff remained concerned about their ability to comply with the code and also meet the three week turnaround for feedback. Another union concern was to ensure the right for staff to print electronically submitted coursework, although this did conflict with directives in some Schools that electronic submission should not result in increased departmental costs. A further union concern related to the ability of the institutional print room to cope with large volume printing a peak deadline times but this was countered as a historical view of the capabilities of the service.

The early phase implementation is currently being evaluated but the institution has decided to continue with the 'third way' approach for electronic submission. This has been translated into policy for 2011/12 but in a way that still allows academic staff to choose how to mark and provide feedback. The decision to maintain the approach, without further amendment, acknowledges the general sense of initiative overload by academic staff. E-submission does represent a major cultural shift in staff assessment practices and our experience suggests that it cannot be achieved without agreeing some form of consensus in approach. The project has also highlighted to strategic management the complexity of the overall coursework submission process and the need to limit change to what is practicable at any point in time.

4. Reflection and recommendations

In reflecting on the case study experience, the institution has made progress towards implementing electronic submission of coursework and to achieving its objectives. The proposal to implement a 'third way' was critical in moving the process forward. However, we are conscious that implementing e-submission is only one aspect of reviewing and improving assessment practices within the institution. Evidence from existing and emerging research supports the need to redesign assessment practices across the whole institution, REAP (2011), and within programmes of study, TESTA (2011). The intention is to continue working with institutional management, academic staff and students to develop practices that benefit all stakeholders.

In recommending how other institutions might approach development of e-submission policy and practice, a key starting point is analysis of the predominant culture and sub-cultures. Acknowledging the increased influence in student power is essential and early inclusion of student leadership does promote better understanding between key stakeholders. The needs of key stakeholders need to align but giving stakeholders the opportunity to vent their concerns is also critical in promoting better understanding. This needs to be conducted in the spirit of listening and moving forward with agreement to minimise concerns. In our case, frequent consultation throughout the various stages of the project did not translate into members of academic staff being aware of the introduction of new policy. Hence, further debate can be expected once any new policy is first implemented. Providing evidence that perceived issues have already been discussed and solutions considered is essential at this stage.

Progress can only be achieved through managing the expectations and understandings of all key stakeholders. Our experience also highlights the need to take an institutional perspective of all initiatives impacting on academic practice, administrative activities and the student experience, at any point in time. Finally, any implementation of e-submission policy and practice needs to be considered in the context of changing assessment practices, in general, and the opportunities that technology provides for alternative approaches to assessment and feedback on assessment.

References

Alvesson, M (2002) Understanding Organizational Culture. London: Sage.

Berquist, W.H. (1992) The Four Cultures of the Academy. San Francisco: Jossey Bass.

HEFCE (2010) Student Perspectives on Technology – demand, perceptions and training needs. Available online at http://www.hefce.ac.uk/pubs/rdreports/2010/rd18_10/

Hepplestone, S., Parkin, H., Irwin, B., Holden, G and Thorpe, L (2010) Technology, Feedback, Action! The impact of learning technology upon students' engagement with their feedback. Available online at http://www.heacademy.ac.uk/assets/EvidenceNet/TFA_report_final.pdf

Land, R. (2001) Agency, context and change in academic development. International Journal for Academic Development, 6 (1), 4-20.

NSF (2009) National Student Forum Annual Report 09. Available online at http://www.bis.gov.uk/assets/biscore/higher-education/docs/n/09-p83-national-student-forum-annual-report-09

NUS (2008) Higher Education Campaign: Mark my words, not my name. Further information available online at http://www.nus.org.uk/en/Campaigns/Higher-Education/Mark-my-words-not-my-name/

NUS (2009) Higher Education Campaign: Assessment feedback. Further information available online at http://www.nus.org.uk/en/Campaigns/Higher-Education/Assessment-feedback-/

REAP (2011) Re-Engineering Assessment Practices in Higher Education. Further information available online at http://www.reap.ac.uk/Home.aspx

TESTA (2011) Transforming the Experience of Students Through Assessment. Further information available online at http://www.testa.ac.uk/.

Tierney, W. G. (1988) Organisational culture in higher education. Journal of Higher Education, 59, (1) 2-21.

Trowler, P. (2008) Cultures and Change in Higher Education, 1 -15. New York: Palgrave MacMillan.

Tools for Evaluating Students' Work in an Interactive (Open) Virtual Space: Case Study of an eLearning Course in an International Network of Universities

Jana Dlouhá, Martin Zahradník, Jiří Dlouhý and Andrew Barton
Charles University Environment Center, Charles University, Prague, Czech Republic

Editorial Commentary
The context of this case study relates to the "third purpose" of universities, after teaching and research, which is their contribution to society. This is explored in a European context where students from Germany and the Czech Republic participated in an open and fully online course. Digital literacy was both a means and a by-product of this course through the use of a shared wiki for student work and interaction. Assessment could thus be based on tracking learning through stages of the students' development, in relation to the topic, by their responses to others in the learning environment and by the development of subsequent versions of their assignment. This paper makes intriguing reading as an experiment in social learning, where the technology both enables and makes transparent the outcomes of community engagement.

Abstract: This article presents a brief analysis of changes in educational practices associated with the "third role" of higher education institutions (HEIs) that are occurring not only at an institutional level, but also within the learning process taking place at lower levels (individual, course, program) and could be effectively combined with the introduction of eLearning methodologies into teaching that stress the social aspects of learning. Teaching in the open space provides the opportunity to use active forms of teaching / learning and creates conditions for social learning. Conceptual and practical shifts would also involve methods of assessment to justify their benefits and stress certain qualities in higher education (HE). Based on these theoretical considerations, practical experience with the eLearning course "Multiple

Jana Dlouhá, Martin Zahradník, Jiří Dlouhý and Andrew Barton

Perspectives on Globalization and Sustainable Development" operated as part of the international Virtual Campus for Sustainable Development (VCSE) eLearning program is analyzed. The method of teaching was geared toward independent and collaborative student work in a wiki environment and the development of key competences necessary to understand and be active in the complex field of sustainability. The authors show how to practically apply the pedagogical principle that educational objectives, methods, learning environments and assessment procedures must be aligned. For assessment, a combination of evaluation tools was introduced, such as rubrics evaluated by teachers and questionnaires completed by the course participants which provided feedback on course outcomes in comparison with its educational goals. The method of assessment focused on "students' approaches to learning" is described, and the possibilities for promoting and evaluating social learning processes that would contribute to the development of capabilities to communicate across disciplinary and academic boundaries within higher education are discussed.

Keywords: higher education, eLearning, competences, social learning, Wiki, assessment

1. Introduction – change of practices in higher education

With regard to their potential engagement in society and active participation in its transition toward sustainability, universities have to develop a third role based on interaction with other societal players, and mutual interdependence with society ("co-evolution" with its systems) (Ferrer-Balas et al., 2009). In this article we will argue that the envisaged change might be applied at an individual level and thus brought into the heart of education - through transformation of the knowledge generation process that will emphasize its social functions, the development of participation and to involve a "system's thinking, joint learning, open communication..." (Lukman et al., 2009). In practice, an expanded set of educational outcomes is required: besides knowledge (that should reside in an individual's head), competences that are developed and are subsequently demonstrated in meaningful practice are important. An operational definition of competences is based on a combination of skills, knowledge and attitudes that are appropriate to particular situations (Dlouhá,

2009a, 2009b); competences relevant to sustainable development (the theme of the course described further on) involve: "competency for using, shaping, handling and sharing different sets of information and knowledge", "competency for dealing with uncertainties and thinking proactively", and "process-oriented and structural knowledge" (Burandt and Barth, 2010).

This perspective is associated with constructivist theories, focusing on the *learning process* as a distinct field, situational understanding of it (the process is affected by a particular situation), and research that is no longer focused on student characteristics such as intelligence, but rather on their individual preferences, perceptions of the learning environment and motivations. This focus brought about not only considerable methodological gains but also possibilities to influence the learning process and resulting student achievements through teacher interventions (Entwistle, 2000).

1.1. Learning approaches

Learning processes started to be researched in Britain and Sweden in the 1970s and the studies were focused on the learning environment factors - these factors are perceived differently by students and result in a combination of student motives and strategies which was defined as student *approaches to learning:* "surface", "deep" and "achieving learning approach" (Biggs, 1987). Research proved that student approaches to learning considerably affect learning processes in terms of their efficiency and have an impact on the final student's performance. The learning environment factors are explored in studies that concentrate on the educational requirements, the quality of the teaching and the nature of the assessment, but also student interests and support, the enthusiasm shown by the instructor and the opportunity for students to manage their own learning process (Richardson, 2009).

New methodologies for assessment of the learning environment and its psychical (motivations) and social determinants were subsequently developed and numerous psychometric measurement techniques based on questionnaires assessing student learning experiences have already been tested so that they can be applied in practice as evaluation instruments for educational management purposes. The interest of researchers is mostly determined by the attempt to improve student performance by influencing in particular the learning environment as an external prerequisite for a good learning process and consequent success.

1.2. Assessment process

Assessment is a rather complex task both at an institutional or system level, and at the level of learning processes. Different factors that play a role in these processes should be aligned: not only educational goals and content, but also tasks and assessment. Evaluators of higher education teaching agree that the most commonly misaligned factor is assessment and "most assessment strategies tend to focus on what is easy to measure rather than what is important." For success in learning, all different aspects of the learning process are relevant – for example, social interactions play a role in which students are engaged when they carry out their tasks, such as collaboration and teamwork, relationships with their tutors, and also learning environment factors. Best teaching assessment practices in higher education should capture these aspects and therefore focus on "critical thinking, problem solving, creativity, curiosity, concern for ethical issues" as well as "breadth and depth of specific knowledge"; they also reflect the "methodologies and standards of evidence used to create that knowledge". Attention paid to these factors is a requirement of active, constructivist pedagogy, but in practice, in most cases assessment is based upon multiple-choice tests or academic essays (Reeves, 2006).

Higher education has therefore many specific features that make the assessment task even more complex than at lower educational levels. Rather ambitious evaluation goals include not only assessment of outcomes, but also reflection of the learning process itself by teachers AND students themselves; assessment techniques comprise peer assessment, self-assessment, authentic assessment and other sophisticated methods. All of these assessment techniques require that students evaluate work of the same kind that they themselves are producing, and thus also obtain experience of realistic evaluation (Sadler, 2005). Besides this, they are aware of assessment criteria that are transparent and could apply to their own performance.

1.3. Social learning perspective

A social learning definition will be used further as an explanatory framework for the case study (Wenger, 2000); it describes this phenomenon as "an interplay between social competence and personal experience; it is a dynamic, two-way relationship between people and social learning systems in which they participate. In this constellation, the necessary competences are negotiated through the experience of direct participation: engagement in joint enterprise requires that members of a community are competent to contribute to it, to interact and mutually reflect on this interaction; and they also share a common repertoire of communal resources such as language, routines, etc. According to Reed, social learning "occurs through social interactions and processes between actors within a social network, either through direct interaction, e.g., conversation, or through other media, e.g., mass media, telephone, or Web 2.0 applications" (Reed et al. 2010). A role for the open virtual space such as Wiki in education is also reported by other authors (Wheeler et al, 2008; Wheeler & Wheeler, 2009).

2. Case study - MPG&SD course in the VCSE network

The Multiple Perspectives on Globalization and Sustainable Development (MPG&SD) course ran over the 2009/2010 European winter semester. The course was part of the international VCSE network of European universities and participated in by students from Germany and the Czech Republic. The course was distant (fully eLearning) and the planned workload was 150 hours (5 credits). Twelve students of the 15 who enrolled successfully completed it.

2.1. Educational goals

In the course, students had to develop three literacies – environmental & SD, academic writing, and ICT literacy. Environmental & SD literacy was related to the theme of the course and students had to learn about environmental problems and sustainable development policies very generally, and study a theme of their choice in more depth. Writing literacy was considered to be an important metacognitive skill necessary to carry out the writing assignment. Students should proceed through all the stages of the academic writing process; their progress from one stage to the next was monitored. ICT literacy was a prerequisite and also a byproduct of learning. Students' written assignments as the main product of the course were displayed in the students' wiki space, and finally, the tutor compiled a Globalization Handbook as a common virtual publication available for a future "generation" of students as a starting point (Dlouhá, 2010). The rules and formal customs of research and academic writing had to be followed while stressing a creative and critical approach.

A wiki environment as an open space for students' creative work on the course themes was used: they wrote their assignments, discussed their content (including a peer review) and shared their views there (Dlouhá & Macháčková-Henderson, 2008; Dlouhá & Dlouhý, 2009). The role of the learning environment was specific; it should stress interdisciplinary aspects of the learning process, and support active learning approaches and solutions. These goals were achieved thanks to its more fluid character which offered different ways of going through content, and provided an interactive character and a three-dimensional structure (hyperlinks opening successive themes).

2.2. Rules and requirements

No online testing occurred (cheating is difficult to prevent in distant education). Students experienced academic discourse and the principles of communication in a community of researchers: its possibilities (freedom of choice of the research theme), rules (research ethics and norms of writing, respect for the critical procedures of a peer review, formal requirements) and limitations (the necessity to narrow the theme of interest and to proceed with discipline and efficiency toards justified conclusions).

The relationship between the different processes could be tracked (peer review versus changes in the article). Moreover, the learning processes could also be assessed – they were documented in the Wiki environment (where the writing process was realized) in the page history. This option allowed a comparison of subsequent versions of the article and was used to analyze the influence of a student's review on the quantity of the text (supposedly affecting its quality) – see Figure 1.

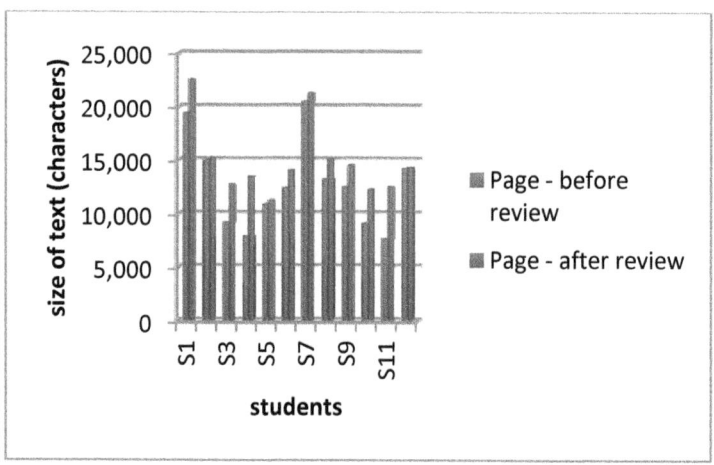

Figure 1: Comparison of student essays in the wiki environment before and after the peer review

The number of bytes before and after the peer review (documented in the page history) was compared; the results showed changes especially in the articles that were underdeveloped before peer review.

The role of communication was important – a negotiated standpoint from participants and a common decision on a hypothetical problem were required. The evidence of communication was available in the fora; it could be analyzed and served as a resource for further research. The mutual peer review process was undertaken in the Wiki space and its results played a role in the quality criterion. The course outcomes were demonstrated in student portfolios which consisted of: fora discussion contributions (evidence available in Moodle), student essays and mutual critical reviews of them (evidence in Wiki).

All actors were actively involved in the learning processes and were in permanent interaction with each other as well as with the learning environment – it was not only a resource base, but also a factor in changing their roles. As subsequent research proved, the electronic environment (the Moodle system) itself helped to monitor student activity, or control the quantity and timing of assignments handed in, and thus influenced the performance of authority in the learning process. The virtual electronic environment thus provided some almost invisible powers and thus took over some functions of the authority that teachers use in face-to-face interactions (Dlouhá, M., 2010).

2.3. The role of, and the tools for assessment

The learning goals in the MPG&SD course were focused on the skills and competences needed for self-regulation of the learning process, such as understanding, critical judgment, complex thinking (awareness of the interdisciplinary context), commitment (the values behind scientific work), and a constructivist and action-oriented approach (in theory and practice). Assessment goals were process, not outcome oriented; the assessment options were adjusted to these goals and closely related to the features and qualities of the articles and other texts produced by students – their essays and all other contributions in fora were carefully analyzed in each stage of the course. New assessment tools for evaluation of the specific qualities mentioned above had to be developed – evaluation rubrics were used for all texts produced in the course. The rubrics assessed to what extent educational goals in terms of (sustainability oriented) competences demonstrated by the specific properties of the texts written by students were met (see Table 1).

Table 1: Example of the assessment rubric for a student's essay – Wiki text (shortened)

Criteria/levels of fulfillment	10	0	Competence under consideration
Content	quality of resources & well-founded argumentation	information is limited; argument is biased	Knowledge (deep)
Focus	strong conclusions, values behind the topic are clear	various themes with no clear priorities, value orientation not certain	Understanding (research question)
Context	wide context & core of the problem identified	narrow context, problems not inter-related	Knowledge (broad)
Clarity	logical structure of the text, clear ideas in sentence, paragraph etc.	ideas unclear, disconnected; structure not logical	Information management
Critical approach	balanced text: opposing views presented	one-sided, demagogic	Critical thinking
Commitment	ethics (writing) & length (text)	ethical principles not satisfactorily respected	Values
Individual input & risk-taking	initiative in researching topic, originality, independent work with resources	no new perspectives; conclusions not original	Action competence
Formal features	respecting academic genre, citation format respected	mixed genre, citation format and ethics insufficient	*Respect for formal requirements*

Assessment tools designed for specific evaluation needs (competences) and online environment options exploited the evidence of the learning outcomes – a portfolio of students' work was transparently available in the learning space.

2.4. Feedback – student perceptions

Because of the complex character of the skills and competences to be developed within the course, the principle of student interactive involvement and the rule that the learning process should be reflected by them was applied (due also to the low number of course teachers/tutors and a presumed lack of evaluation objectivity), while particular attention was paid to the students' reflection of the learning environment, requirements and outcomes.

Students' perceptions of the academic quality of courses in distance education are (according to relevant research) strongly associated with the approaches to studying that they adopt on those courses (Richardson, 2009). Moreover, by comparing desirable educational goals in terms of competences with characteristics of the students' approaches we have identified a deep study approach, in contrast to a surface approach, as the necessary condition for the development of desirable skills and competences. The deep study approach can be described as "looking for meaning in the matter being studied and relating it to other experiences and ideas with a critical approach. Students adopting a deep approach aim to understand the subject and are intrinsically interested in, and derive enjoyment from, studying. A surface approach can be thought of as a reliance on roteLearning and memorization in isolation to other ideas. Surface learners perceive the task of learning as an external imposition and they are externally motivated. They typically treat parts of the subject as separate entities and fail to integrate topics into a coherent whole." (Duff, 2004).

It has been argued that students must usually "take a deep learning approach in order to develop an effective understanding of the multidimensional meaning of the complex topic of sustainability or sustainable development" because complexity of the problem itself requires an active approach and deep understanding (von Blottnitz, 2006).

To assess the extent to which students applied a deep/surface approach to studying, the standardized Experiences of Teaching and

Learning Questionnaire (ETLQ) was used to explore student approaches to learning and studying (Richardson, 2009). Even though the questionnaire explores solely the process of learning, the nature of this process relates strongly to final educational outcomes, as has been proved by several studies (Entwistle et al., 2000; Duff, 2003; Mattick et al., 2004). At the same time, researchers conclude that the *studying approach* is in turn influenced by the context of learning (Duff, 2004; Parpala et al., 2010). The MPG&SD course is designed with the goal of supporting the development of students' competences using web 2.0 tools in an eLearning environment and we expected that the strong emphasis put on their involvement in communication and self-directed action will be associated with a deep study approach in the process of learning. The ETLQ questionnaire designed by Entwistle to distinguish different student approaches was applied to verify this assumption: we used its short 18 item version that considers four dimensions/approaches to learning: the deep approach, monitored studying, organized studying, effort management, and the surface approach (Mattick et al., 2004). The first three of them relate to desirable ways of studying and refer to deep involvement in the learning process characterized by interest and understanding.

The results of testing are presented in Table 2 - students apparently refer to the prevailing deep approach and reject the surface learning statements. This inquiry (application of a quantitative questionnaire to a low number of students) was based on the application of a standardized tool whose validity and reliability has been proved by previous surveys (Mattick et al., 2004; Parpala et al., 2010; Duff, 2004). A median was used instead of a mean to represent students' opinions as a more appropriate measure from such a low number of respondents. The fact that most of the positive statements resulted in *4 = agree* and the prevailing answer to the surface approach was *2 = disagree* supports the hypothesis about encouraging course environment, i.e. context of learning.

Color scale	1	1.5	2	2.5	3	3.5	4	4.5	5

Color scale used in all following tables: 5-point Likert scale (from Strongly disagree = 1 point to Strongly agree = 5 points)

Table 2: Results obtained in final standardized Experiences of Teaching and Learning (12 students)

Indicate to what extent you agree with the following statement...	Data 2009/ 2010 *median*	Demonstration of the learning approach
I have usually tried to understand for myself the meaning of what we had to learn	4	DA: Intention to understand for oneself
In reading for this course, I've tried to find out for myself exactly what the author means	4	DA: Intention to understand for oneself
In making sense of new ideas, I have often related them to practical or real life contexts	4	DA: Relating ideas (including constructivist learning)
Ideas I've come across in my academic reading often set me off on long chains of thought	3.5	DA: Relating ideas (including constructivist learning)
I've looked at evidence carefully to reach my own conclusion about what I'm studying	4	DA: Use of evidence
It has been important for me to follow the argument, or to see the reasons behind things	4.5	DA: Use of evidence
When I've been communicating ideas, I've thought over how well I've got my points across (so that others understood)	4	MS: Monitoring generic skills
I've tried to find better ways of tracking down relevant information in this subject	3	MS: Monitoring generic skills
I have been revising the work I've done to check my reasoning and see that it makes sense	4	MS: Monitoring understanding
If I've not understood things well enough when studying, I've tried a different approach	4	MS: Monitoring understanding

Indicate to what extent you agree with the following statement...	Data 2009/ 2010 median	Demonstration of the learning approach
Concentration has not usually been a problem for me, unless I've been really tired	4	OS: Concentration
I have generally put a lot of effort into my studying	5	OS: Effort
On the whole, I've been quite systematic and organized in my studying	4	OS: Organised studying
I've organized my study time carefully to make the best use of it	4	OS: Time management
Much of what I've learned seems no more than lots of unrelated bits and pieces in my mind	2	SA: Fragmented knowledge
I've often had trouble in making sense of the things I have to remember	2.5	SA: Memorizing without understanding
I've just been going through the motions of studying without seeing where I'm going	2	SA: Unreflective studying
I've tended to take as guaranteed what we've been taught without questioning it much	2	SA: Unthinking acceptance

Questionnaire (ETLQ): DA = Deep approach, MS = Monitoring studying, OS = Organized studying and effort management, SA = Surface approach. 5 item scale, 1 = strongly disagree, 5 = strongly agree

This finding was further supported by the results of a questionnaire designed to explore specific competences developed through the course in a post-course survey using a 5-point Likert scale. The answers were also compared with students' expectations about achieving the competences in a similar pre-course survey and thus provided feedback on the course achievements related to the learning outcomes expected by students entering the virtual environment. For this subjective reflection on the degree to which students developed a certain competence or have found some process of learning useful see Figures 2 and 3, and for those who are interested in detailed wording see Tables 3 and 4. Comparison with an objective assessment of students' achievements undertaken by the teacher using an evaluation rubric (see above) was not done due to non-comparable categories used in both cases; nevertheless, visible outcomes in terms of a portfolio of students' work (essays, peer reviews, discussions) could not be achieved without using the surveyed competences in practice.

Students' perception of learning outcomes in terms of competences is in accordance with findings about the good quality of the learning process (manifested as students' approaches to learning). These findings might support the hypothesis that the method of teaching used in MPG&SD was appropriate for sustainability-oriented education and the high expectations placed on social learning processes in a virtual space were, at least in this limited case, justified. We can state that an open virtual learning environment that promotes independent work, communication and social interaction fulfilled the teacher's and students' expectations to a great extent.

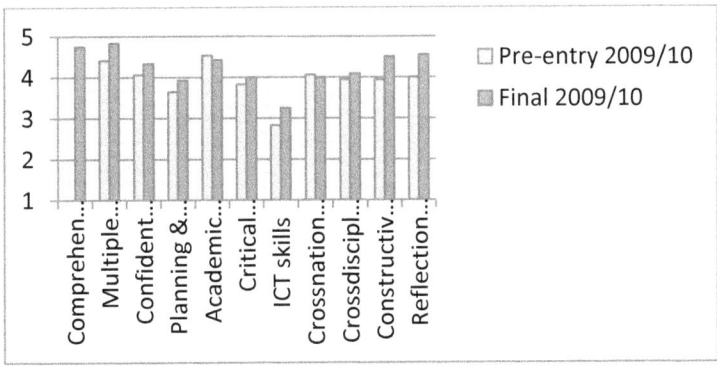

Figure 2: Results obtained in the final questionnaire developed for assessment of competences

Comparison of means with relevant questions in the pre-entry questionnaire (see these questions in Table 3.)

Table 3: Questions in final questionnaire developed for assessment of competences.

Learning Outcomes	Data 2009/2010		
Indicate to what extent do you agree with the following statement:	Description of the skill / competence	Final 12 students median	Expectations Pre-entry 15 students median
I would be able to explain the main topics of the seminar to a third person.	Comprehensive understanding	5	
I increased my ability to be able to understand and interpret global issues from multiple perspectives (disciplinary perspectives e.g. sociology, economics, philosophy etc).	Multiple perspectives	5	5
I developed confidence in my own ability to express my own well-informed arguments in globalization and sustainable development debates.	Confident argumentation	4.5	4
I increased my ability to plan my time and study independently.	Planning & studying	4	4
I developed my ability to write texts which express my points clearly.	Academic writing	4	5
I developed my capacity to evaluate whether information is biased or credible.	Evaluation of info	4	4
I developed my computer skills.	ICT	4	3
I developed my ability to communicate with people from other countries.	Cross-national communication	4	4

Learning Outcomes	Data 2009/2010		
Indicate to what extent do you agree with the following statement:	Description of the skill / competence	Final 12 students median	Expectations Pre-entry 15 students median
I developed my ability to study and communicate with people from other disciplinary backgrounds.	Cross-disciplinary communication	4	4
I developed my ability to provide constructive criticism on fellow students' work.	Constructive criticism	4.5	4
I developed my ability to reflect on the quality of my own work.	Reflection on own work	5	4

Results compared with previous year of the course and with relevant questions in pre-entry questionnaire

In the pre-entry questionnaire, modified wording was used: "My expectations of the course can be characterised by the following sentences …" "I expect to…"

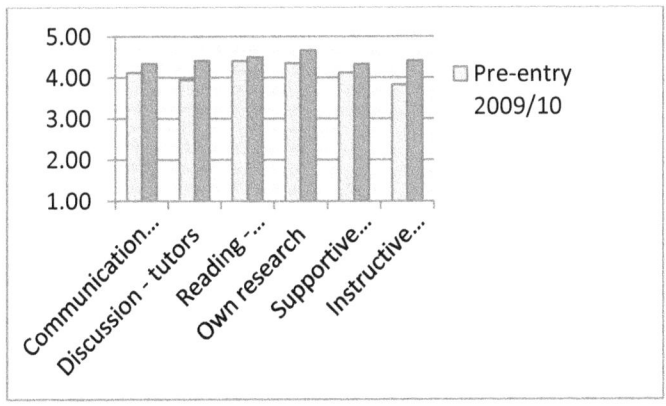

Figure 3: Results received in the final questionnaire developed for assessment of the learning process

Comparison of means with relevant questions in pre-entry questionnaire (see these questions in Table 4.)

Table 4: Questions in the final questionnaire developed for assessment of the learning process.

Learning Process	Data 2009/2010		
Indicate to what extent do you agree with the following statement:	Description of the skill / competence	Final 12 students	Expectations Pre-entry 15 students
		median	median
I developed new ideas and learned new information through communication with my fellow students.	Communication - students	4	4
I developed new ideas and learned new information through discussion with my tutors.	Discussion - tutors	5	4
I developed new ideas and learned new information through reading provided materials.	Reading - provided materials	5	5
I developed new ideas and learned new information through researching my own topics of interest within the course.	Own research	5	5
My tutor helped me to find my own answers about the content of the course when I needed it.	Supportive assistance	4	4
My tutor provided answers to my questions about the content of the course when I need it.	Instructive assistance	5	4

Results compared with previous year of the course and with relevant questions in the pre-entry questionnaire.

3. Discussion

Qualitative feedback is more appropriate for courses such as MPG&SD. It provided information about prior knowledge of the course topic, detailed feedback on eLearning tools, course content, discussion topics, workload, and satisfaction with students' own performances. Regarding evaluation of trained skills and competences, we can identify the following items as what students perceived they gained: language skills (English – all students were non-native speakers), writing (by creating their own wiki article, developing the proper formal structure of an article, use of citations and references, a true peer review process, communication: *discuss and consider other opinions,* and time management.

Looking at students' open comments on course quality we can again find mostly positive reactions like: "In total I really liked this course and I am happy that I participated in it. This course I really found fun to handle. Hope to participate in other course like it." The last comment was elicited from a specific statement: "I would recommend this course to my colleagues/fellow students." Eight students agreed, while 4 of the 12 provided no response. Critical opinions also appeared. The intellectual demands of the course were perceived as high. In addition, the whole course was seen as too time-consuming and sometimes deadlines were not 100% clear. Nevertheless, the positive reaction to the course environment resulted in a unanimous appreciation of the tutors' involvement, which is always crucial for the creation of a well-functioning eLearning course.

Other researchers combine the results of an analysis of learning approaches with other analytical tools focused on students' reactions to teaching. This is only possible when a certain number of students is analyzed. For example, Noel Entwistle, Velda McCune and Jenny Hounsell (2002) report on research that looks for relationships between approaches to studying and the teaching-learning environment carried out within several courses. They find the concepts and categories used to describe general differences in studying to be a valuable analytical framework that allows consideration of how individuals study and shows how various aspects of a teaching-learning environment may affect student engagement in the course. Thus, the effects of the teaching-learning environment, as perceived by the students, in terms of their deep approach to it might be assessed to a certain extent. In addition, students' perceptions of a particular course might be compared with their general approach to studying, so that a pedagogical effect would be indicated. These authors concluded that the ETLQ questionnaires are working effectively and are able to detect changes in approaches to studying depending on changes in course design aimed at enhancing teaching-learning environments to support high-quality learning, or compare the responses of students who had first-hand experience of the innovation with those who had not.

In general, the deep studying approach should result in good quality outcomes and academic performance (Entwistle et al., 2000; Duff, 2003). We have not overestimated the results of the evaluation of on our course with a limited number of participants due to which we were not able to proceed with a deeper statistical analysis; we have simply presented feedback on possible evaluation tools that could be used for the assessment of social learning processes that give educational outcomes different to those achieved in traditional HE settings.

4. Conclusion – the applied social learning concept in an eLearning course

The HE course presented as a case study is a model of the applied concept of social learning in eLearning. In the MPG&SD course, students had to learn from the social environment with the support of an electronic environment. The manner of involvement should follow the principles of (and communication in) the academic community in general; the teaching method used and the eLearning environment selected were mediators of the educational aims. The eLearning environment was flexible enough to provide the options required, and, moreover, it provided evidence so that the learning processes could be researched in different stages, as the work of the students was continuously documented. Evidence of participants' contributions in the forum discussion space provided the opportunity to observe the social aspects of scientific work and the principles of academic dialogue – the roles of participants in the dialogue, the distribution of authority, possibilities of communication across boundaries, the added value of a multicultural environment, etc. The research dimension was highlighted in an eLearning environment that makes external evaluation possible.

Some of explorations undertaken and experiences obtained would not be possible without the multicultural and interdisciplinary learning environment that was achieved within the VCSE international network of cooperation. International collaboration generally promotes intercultural understanding, fosters the exchange of information on global problems, supports the transfer of experiences and provides a broader sustainability context (Vann et al., 2006).

The course represented an experiment in teaching, with well documented and transparent outcomes that were tenable with regards to academic skills – student academic essays compiled in the final edition of the Globalization Handbook, and their reviews of colleagues' articles in the discussion part of the wiki page (and also numerous fora contributions). It was an example of the applied "community of practice" model in teaching where the learning environment played a crucial role, especially with its social aspects (actors and their roles, communication tools and means), but also the information management options, etc. The social learning methodology – teaching through involvement in the community, accepting and applying its discourse – brought about an educational experience that should be explored further.

References

Biggs, J.B. (1987) Student Approaches to Learning and Studying. Research Monograph. Australian Council for Educational Research Ltd., Radford House, Australia, 14–19.

von Blottnitz, H. (2006) Promoting active learning in sustainable development: experiences from a 4th year chemical engineering course. Journal of Cleaner Production 14(9-11), 916-923.

Burandt, S., Barth, M. (2010) Learning settings to face climate change. Journal of Cleaner Production 18(7), 659–665.

Dlouhá, J., Mácháčková-Henderson, L. (2008) ELearning as an opportunity for virtual mobility and competence development within European Universi-

ties. In: Williams R; Remenyi, D. (ed.) The Proceedings of the 7th European Conference on eLearning (ECEL). NR Reading: Academic Publishing Limited. Book 1, pp. 297–307
Dlouhá, J., Dlouhý, J. (2009) Use of Wiki Tools for Raising the Communicative Aspect of Learning. In: Remenyi D. (ed.) Proceedings of the 8th European Conference on eLearning. NR Reading: Academic Conferences Ltd. 165-173
Dlouhá, J. (2009a) General educational qualities and the term "competence". Envigogika 4(1) Online. Retrieved on 2009-06-16, from http://envigogika.cuni.cz/index.php/cs/texty/20091/299-obecne-vzdlavaci-kvality-a-pojem-kompetence
Dlouhá, J. (2009b) Competences in environmental education. Envigogika 4(1) Online. Retrieved on 2009-06-16, from http://envigogika.cuni.cz/index.php/cs/texty/20091/300-kompetence-v-environmentalnim-vzdlani-
Dlouhá, J. (2010) Globalisation Risks and Opportunities. VCSEWiki. Online. Retrieved on 2010-08-31, from http://www.czp.cuni.cz/vcsewiki/index.php?title=Globalisation_Risks_and_Opportunities&oldid=1350
Dlouhá, M. (2010) Authority in virtual education. Charles University in Prague, FSV, ISS, Praha.
Duff, A. (2003) Quality of Learning on an MBA Programme: The Impact of Approaches to Learning on Academic Performance. Educational Psychology 23, 123-139
Duff, A. (2004) The Revised Approaches to Studying Inventory (RASI) and its Use in Management Education. Active learning in Higher education 56(5), p. 57
Entwistle, N. (2000). Promoting deep learning through teaching and assessment: conceptual frameworks and educational contexts. *TLRP conference, Leicester.*
Entwistle, N., Tait, H. & McCune, V. (2000) Patterns of Response to an Approaches to Studying Inventory Across Contrasting Groups and Contexts. European Journal of the Psychology of Education 15, 33-48
Entwistle, N., McCune, V., & Hounsell, J. (2002). Approaches to studying and perceptions of university teaching-learning environments: Concepts, measures and preliminary findings. *Enhancing Teaching and Learning Environments in Undergraduate Courses Occasional Report, 1.*
Ferrer-Balas, D., Buckland, H., de Mingo, M. (2009) Explorations on the University's role in society for sustainable development through a systems transition approach. Case-study of the Technical University of Catalonia (UPC). Journal of Cleaner Production 17(12), 1075-1085.

Lukman, R., Krajnc, D., Glavic, P. (2009) Fostering collaboration between universities regarding regional sustainability initiatives - the University of Maribor. Journal of Cleaner Production 17(12), 1143-1153.

Mattick, K., Dennis, I. & Bligh, J. (2004) Approaches to learning and studying in medical students: validation of a revised inventory and its relation to student characteristics and performance. Medical Education 38(5), 535-543

Parpala, A., Lindblom-Ylänne, S., Komulainen, E., Litmanen, T. & Hirsto, L. (2010) Students' Approaches to Learning and their Experiences of the Teaching-learning Environment in Different Disciplines. British Journal of Educational Psychology 80, 269-282

Reed, M. S., A. C. Evely, G. Cundill, I. Fazey, J. Glass, A. Laing, J. Newig, B. Parrish, C. Prell, C. Raymond, and L. C. Stringer (2010) What is social learning? *Ecology and Society* **15**(4): r1. [online] URL: http://www.ecologyandsociety.org/vol15/iss4/resp1/

Reeves, T.C. (2006) How do you know they are learning? The importance of alignment in higher education. International Journal of Learning Technology, 2(4), 294–309.

Richardson, J.T. (2009) Face-to-face versus online tutoring support in humanities courses in distance education. Arts and Humanities in Higher Education 8(1), 69.

Sadler, R.D. (2005) Interpretations of criteria-based assessment and grading in higher education. Assessment & Evaluation in Higher Education 30(2), 175–194.

Vann, J., Pacheco, P., Motloch, J. (2006) Cross-cultural education for sustainability: development of an introduction to sustainability course. Journal of Cleaner Production 14(9-11), 900-905.

Wenger, E. (2000) Communities of practice and social learning systems. Organization 7(2), 225.

Wheeler, S., Yeomans, P., Wheeler, D. (2008) The good, the bad and the wiki: Evaluating student-generated content for collaborative learning. *British Journal of Educational Technology*, 2008, *39*(6), 987–995.

Wheeler, S., Wheeler, D. (2009) Using wikis to promote quality learning in teacher training. *Learning, Media and Technology*, 2009, Vol. 34, No. 1, March, 1-10

Mutlimodal Teaching Through ICT Education: An e-Twinning Program as a Case Study of Intercultural Exchange

Paraskevi Kanari and Georgios Potamias
National Kapodistrian University of Athens, Greece

Editorial Commentary
The potential of e-learning to reduce transactional distance and enable cultural and learning exchange is drawn out clearly in this case study, located in Greece but involving schools both in Greece and in Poland. The richness of images in relation to learning is one of the drivers of this project, images which can so easily be shared through educational technologies using multimedia. The paper sets out a brief summary of an intercultural project between the two schools which aimed to develop critical visual literacy as well as an appreciation of varying cultural heritage. The role of the technology here was as mediator of experience and legend, agent of cultural exchange, both visual and textual, and social channel for connecting otherwise isolated students.

Abstract: Multimodality is a key factor in promoting knowledge through multidimensional aspects in an approach, determined by social environment. In the approach presented, school is a part of an accepted social context. This paper shows that development of critical visual literacy via ICT education and e-learning combined with conventional activities can be an innovative multidisciplinary approach for the development of pedagogical projects. The cultural program in particular presented, which was carried out in the island of Spetses in Greece, was integrated in this approach. The ultimate goal was to create a film transfer of a local legend by the students of Spetses' junior high an area culturally challenged. The program was integrated to an e-twinning project (e-learning European exchange program) concerning revitalizing local legends through e-learning, filmmaking, teaching local History through French language and intercultural exchange with the cooperation of two European schools, one in the Greek island of Spetses and one in

Chorwovie in Poland. Through this e-learning project the students carried out a different multimodal approach of French Language and Local Culture achieving the development of their creativity and imagination through cultural e-interactivity and their cognitive and social awareness as well.

Keywords: multimodal approach, social semiotics, e-twinning, cinema, local history, public school

1. Multimodality and cinematographic education

In a time of intense semiotic, visual stimulus (Cocula & Peyroutet 1999: 10) (medias, computer, cinema) an educational system that stays attached to the "ex cathedra"(traditional frontal) method of teaching is impossible to correspond to the interests and needs of modern day students and it is inevitably boring in comparison to their every day learning experiences. The case of critical visual literacy which is defined as the ability of understanding, decoding, producing and criticizing visual messages is in our times more indispensable than ever (Kress& Van Leeuwen 1996:3; Pleios 2005:238). According to Sankey (2005: 2) a widespread development of critical visual literacy is necessary in order to cultivate and enhance the ability of reading and semiologically decoding both a text and an image as a whole or separately. Schirato & Yell (1996: 209) add that in western societies, a literate person will be considered primary one that can identify, read, analyze and develop a wide variety of visual signs and interactive stimulus. Researches on imagery and its semiotic sustainability (Levie & Lentz 1982) prove that images can largely promote teaching and social based knowledge. The most important advantages of teaching through the use of images are:

- The images are stocked easily in long term memory, creating information as connecting parts or meanings in human memory.
- Images provoke a wide range of reactions like the rise and wakening of imagination. They create connections; they promote and cultivate creative thinking and abstract imagination.

- The readers or users of teaching material prefer illustrative material for its higher information quality.
- The combination of imagery and text is more effective in promoting comprehension than the text alone.
- The images can be useful in understanding and learning abstract meanings that can be hardly expressed with words.
- Images can help mentally or physically challenged students in learning efficiently.
- The teaching use of images is proved more effective when teaching is connected with the flexible and combined use of internet; computer enhanced virtual environments and cinema (Kress 2005: 11-12).

The role of the teacher is to create an educational and pedagogical environment that could encourage students' critical thinking towards imagery (images of whatever status or quality) as the increasing number of visual stimulus make students confuse reality with the virtual reality of computer or visual empowered artificial environments (Joly 2005:447; Smyrneos 2008:214). Therefore, the development of critical visual literacy is imperative for modern students and generally citizens.

The teaching via cinema, the cinematographic education, is strongly attached to multi-modal education (Jacquinot 1977:27; Tardy 1973:27). Cinema and moving pictures, more traditional semiotic means of education than modern computer empowered visualizations, can be the source of multiple teaching activities with parallel analysis of images, text and sound. The ultimate goal in this approach is the promotion of multiple communicative and sensory interactions between students (Régis 2009: 9).

The cinematographic education is necessary for the understanding of modern multimodal media world. The multimodal cinematographic teaching, based on image, promotes the ability of:

- Using an inexhaustible source of visual material.
- Reading, criticizing and decoding the multiple diversity, function and temporality of visual material.

- Using rationally electronic equipment (computer, video, cinema) and visual means for gathering and managing critical information.
- Using multimedia applications in order to create multimodal contexts and interactive compositions (combination of image- text- sound).
- Promoting and presenting cinematographic creations in an informative sustainable way (Yakoumatou 2006:74-75; Semoglou 2005:18; The New London Group 1996).

Despite the objections towards developing powerful and sophisticated criteria that can be theoretically able to promote students' understanding of visual communication (Barthes 1977:88; Baudinet – Mondzain 1990:15), the need for promoting multimodal interactive teaching is urgent in modern day school.

An effort for the creation of a school curriculum that can empower the management of critical information has been carried out in many countries. Such curriculums theoretically consider very important the cultivation of metacognitive skills, the ability of managing critically important knowledge (Greek Institute of Pedagogy, 1998). Since the development of the internet has given students access to an inexhaustible source of visual information, with the risk of confusion between valid knowledge and useless information, it is imperative to encourage the integration of a more visually aesthetic critical education in a modern curriculum (Barnett 2000:22; Gonnet 1997:17).

Although it would be an exaggeration to assert the primacy of visual literacy, it is generally accepted that many students accept willingly the integration of visual material, in order to support and enrich textual and non-textual material in a holistically empowered semiotic context (Semoglou 2005:564-565).

Very recently, the introduction of interactive blackboards, and generally rich visual educational means (dvd, internet videos, use of youtube or teachtube videos in the classroom) has an innovative and revolutionary impact in the heart of modern school ethos. The students are excited from the immediacy, audacity and relevance of illustrations and visual reproductions of all forms. However, the teachers should be very cautious and concerned towards not only the semiotic informative quality and pedagogical content of the imagery used but also towards their ability to use, manipulate and successfully manage the inexhaustible source of visual information (Sankey 2005:10; Van Leeuwen & Jewitt 2001:107).

2. Application of the theory in an educational context

In the context of multimodal cinematographic education, a cultural program was carried out in the island of Spetses in Greece during the school year 2007-2008. The ultimate goal of this program was to create a film transfer of a local legend by the students of Spetses' junior high (students from 12 to 15 years old), an area culturally and educationally challenged. Spetses is a small island of 5000 inhabitants with long and rich history but with poor cultural activity, due to its isolation, especially in winter time. The authors took part in the design, the implementation and the evaluation of this program, mentoring students and recording every step of its development through the e-platforms of the e-twining program. The results of the program were presented virtually in the e-twinning e-platform and in a cultural event hosted by the municipal authorities of the town.

In the case study presented in this paper, multimodality is presented as an educational means of holistically enhancing intercultural and social awareness in school. Thus multimodality in praxis affects positively not only educational competencies of students but also the social context as a whole.

The program was integrated to an e-twinning project (e-learning European exchange program) concerning the revival of local legends through e-learning, ICT education, filmmaking, teaching local History and intercultural exchange. In this case two European schools cooperated, one in the Greek island of Spetses and one in Chorwovie of Poland.

The purpose of the program was discovering and revitalizing local legends of each area and exchanging creatively this cultural experience with the other school. The program was divided in three parts. In the first part, each school presented itself by writing and uploading an e-twinning portrait of their school and of themselves. In the second part the students tried to discover various local legends by asking their parents or the elders of their community. After selecting amongst the amount of legends discovered, each school presented the first part (the beginning) of one or more legends and the other school tried to imagine the end of the story. Written activities in French concerning any given legend were given to students (description of the main character, developing language enhancing activities such as crosswords with the new vocabulary etc.). The Greek legend turned into a film was entitled in French language: "La vieille dame et le paon" ("the old lady and the peacock). In the third part, the end of the story was given to the students. The presentation of schools, the comments and the e-communication between students was in French. The Polish school chose to present the legends through the use of Microsoft's power point programme. The Greek school chose to present its legend through a short film.

Through this e-learning project the students carried out a different multimodal approach of Culture and History achieving not only the development of their creativity and imagination through cultural e-interactivity, but their cognitive and social awareness as well. E-learning and visual enhancing tools promoted the breaking of social and educational barriers through intercultural activities in two culturally challenged European areas

2.1. General aims of the cultural e-twinning program

- Approaching visual literacy through cinema and its techniques
- The production of a short film.
- Opening school towards other culture and mentalities (Polish legends)
- Opening school towards local society.

- Developing of communicative skills in a common language, as "lingua franca", the French language.
- Considering a foreign language (French) as an empowering tool of communication and cultural exchange.

2.2. Specific purposes

- Getting to know Greek and French cinema.
- Sharpening the creativity and imagination of students with exercises and games (role playing games, brainstorming and creativity games).
- Exercising creative writing through writing a scenario.
- Finding and cultivating students' talents and developing responsibility towards class and community.
- Creating a short film as a final product of the project
- Learning a foreign language (French) through multimodal approach.
- Approaching two different cultures and environments (an old miners' region in Poland and a summer resort in Greece).

2.3. Results

- Students got to know unknown areas of cinema and developed their critical thinking towards cinematographic art.
- Students got to know legends and fairy tales of their native place.
- Development of the creativity and imagination of students and teachers as well.
- Constructive use of students' free time and creation of new educative stimulus.
- Development of students' responsibility with the assignment of specific tasks and keeping a specific time plan.
- Improvement of students' communicative skills in French. Using a foreign language outside classroom, in order to fulfill communicative needs was a realistic goal.
- Approach of a different culture and mentality.

- Creation of a short film based on a local legend.
- Presentation of the film in local community as a meta-result of the project in the end of the school year.

2.4. Final evaluation

The program promoted the integration of social and cognitive challenged students in two different countries: Socially isolated students had an opportunity to work in group activities and carry out more interesting and stress-free tasks (isolation due to personal, family or even linguistic problems, e.g. children of immigrants with inadequate literacy).Through this intercultural pedagogical experience, students became more "mature" by increasing their social skills. The school, a place of academic knowledge, usually detached from social context, became an integrated part of society. The research of local history and mythology led to an active acquisition of knowledge based on the given social context. Finally through film making, students and educators revaluated their cultural inheritance by discovering the best sites and traditional abandoned constructions of their island for shooting the film, in order to choose places for the scenes of the film (old houses turned into museums, old coffeehouses). E-learning became a social power tool that provoked educational awareness and cultural interchange. The case study presented in this paper sets an example of how modern innovative multimodal educational approaches, sponsored by European intercultural programmes and combined with traditional pedagogy, can enhance cultural literacy in educationally and culturally challenged areas.

3. Acknowledgements

We would like to thank the National Scholarship Fund of Greece for its support during our research. We would also like to address our gratitude to the people of the island of Spetses for its help and support during the film making.

Referenccs

Barnett, R. (2000) Realizing the university in an age of super-complexity, SRHE/OU, Buckingham

Barthes, R. (1977) Rhetoric of the image, Hill and Wang, New York.

Baudinet –Mondzain, M.J. (1990) "Icone", Les motions philosophiques, t.1, Presses Universitaires de France, Paris.
Cocula, B. & Peyroutet, C. (1999) Sémantique de l'image, Editions Delagrave, Paris.
Gonnet, G. (1997) Education et Media, Presses Universitaires de France, Paris.
Greek Institute of Pedagogy (1998) Interdisciplinary Curriculum, Greek Pedagogic Institute, Athens.
Jacquinot, G. (1977) Image et pédagogie : Analyse sémiologique du film à intention didactique, Presses Universitaires de France, Paris.
Joly, M. (2005) A propos de la formation à la lecture de l'image et à son analyse : entre le diable et l'ineffable in Semoglou, K. (2005) Image and Child, Macedonia University Press, Athens.
Kress, G. (2005) *Imagination, the world of images and the new media* in Semoglou, K. (2005), Image and Child, Macedonia University Press, Athens.
Kress, G., Van Leeuwen, T. (1996) Reading Images. The Grammar of Visual Design, Routledge, London.
Levie, W. H. and Lentz, R. (1982) *"Effects of text illustrations: a review of research"*, Educational Communication and Technology Journal, No. 30, 195-232, Sage Publications, New York.
Pleios, G. (2005) Civilization of Image and Education: The role of Iconic Ideology, Polytropon, Athens.
Régis, C. (2009) *"La lecture de l'image ne s'improvise pas"*, Les français dans le monde, No. 364, pp. 29-31.
Sankey, M. (2005) "Considering visual literacy when designing instruction" [online] University of Southern Queensland from:www.usq.edu.au/users/sankey/Resources/article0602.pdf (accessed on 15/07/2006)
Schirato, T. and Yell, S. (1996) Communication & Cultural Literacy: An Introduction, Allen & Unwin Pty Ltd, St.Leonard.
Semoglou, K. (2005) Image and Child, Macedonia University Press, Athens.
Smyrneos, A. (2008) The didactic of History, Grigoris Publications, Athens.
Tardy, M. (1973) Le professeur et les images, Presses Universitaires de France, Paris.
The New London Group (1996) "A pedagogy of Multiliteracies. Designing Social Futures", [online], www. Thenewlondongroup.com (accessed on 07/07/2007)
Van Leeuwen, T. & Jewitt, C. (2001) Handbook of Image Analysis, Sage, London.

www.ingramcontent.com/pod-product-compliance
Ingram Content Group UK Ltd.
Pitfield, Milton Keynes, MK11 3LW, UK
UKHW022212230426
12048UKWH00016BA/791